AL BURIAN

NO APOCALYPSE

NO APOCALYPSE
PUNK, POLITICS & THE GREAT AMERICAN WEIRDNESS
SELECTED WRITING FROM PUNK PLANET, HEARTATTACK & THE SKELETON

AL BURIAN * 2000 - 2019 *

THIS EDITION © MICROCOSM PUBLISHING, 2019
FIRST EDITION, 3000 COPIES, FIRST PUBLISHED APRIL, 2019

ISBN 978-1-62106-521-0
THIS IS MICROCOSM #237
COVER BY OSKA WALD
BOOK DESIGN BY JOE BIEL & OSKA WALD

FOR A CATALOG, WRITE OR VISIT:
MICROCOSM PUBLISHING
2752 N WILLIAMS AVE.
PORTLAND, OR 97227
(503) 799-2698
MICROCOSMPUBLISHING.COM

LIBRARY OF CONGRESS CATALOGING-IN-PUBLICATION DATA

NAMES: BURIAN, AL, AUTHOR.
TITLE: NO APOCALYPSE : PUNK, POLITICS, AND THE GREAT AMERICAN WEIRDNESS/AL BURIAN
DESCRIPTION: FIRST EDITION. | PORTLAND, OR : MICROCOSM PUBLISHING, 2019.
IDENTIFIERS: LCCN 2018033616 | ISBN 9781621069294 (PBK.)
SUBJECTS: LCSH: BURIAN, AL. | PUNK ROCK MUSICIANS -- UNITED STATES.
CLASSIFICATION: LCC ML 420.B8837 A3 2019 | DDC 306.4/84260973--dc23
LC RECORD AVAILIBLE AT https://lccn.loc.gov/2018033616

14⁹⁵
NEW
1C9

NO APOCALYPSE

PUNK, POLITICS AND THE GREAT AMERICAN WEIRDNESS

AL BURIAN

* MICROCOSM PUBLISHING *
PORTLAND, OR

CONTENTS

INTRODUCTION 7

ILL FITTING SUPERHERO OUTFIT

ILL OUTFITS ... 16
JACKSONVILLE, FL 1999 ... 18
END TIMES, CHICAGO 24
TEETH FALLING OUT ... 30
AMERICAN CUISINE 37
NO DOUBT 45
SPACE SHUTTLE T-SHIRT 52
USA AT WAR 58
COMICS AND REVIEWS ... 66
THANKSGIVING 72
MANITOBA ... 83
LAS VEGAS 86
BLACK SABBATH GREYHOUND CHRISTMAS..87
OPIATE OF THE MASSES
VS. MASSES OF OPIATES 94

AMERICAN VOTER ... 103

MC DONALDS FINDS
MISSING INGREDIENT ... 110

ROAD RAGE ...115

ROME LOPE 119

STORAGE SPACES ...123

DO NOT SWALLOW CONTENTS

Y2K 136

ROME, 1984 ... 140

SYNOPSIZER ... 147

PUNK OVER 30 / DEAD PUNKS ...152

MARRIAGE ... 156

HOME IN THE CITY ... 166

RESIGNATION ...173

Q: HOW'S YOUR SKELETON?

DR. PAZMINSKI, CHIROPRACTOR ...180

IRON MAIDEN, PIECE OF MIND ...184

ETERNAL RETURN 187

INTRODUCTION

The Oncoming Cataclysmic End is a deep and integral part of the American psyche. It is always just around the corner, burbling beneath the surface, unspoken. Or whispered. Or even screamed out loud. America has a great tradition of over-amplified End Times prosthelytizing, not limited to hardcore punk, with its endless cavalcade of mushroom clouds, starving children, fascist multinational corporations, and environmental degradation. To be without that sense of impending doom, to have the thought cross your mind that *maybe this is it and things will just go on like this*—that is the end of history, the end of possibility.

I moved to Chicago in the summer of 2000 with little money to my name and a pretty standard set of goals: I was chasing after love (the relationship was over within a few months, but it held together long enough for us to split the cost of the U-Haul west) and playing in a band. I was also the self-publisher of a well-regarded personal fanzine; at a copy shop I ran off a few copies, hoping to turn a fast buck by consigning them at Quimby's bookstore, thus transforming $10 in copies into about $14 within a few weeks, or possibly months. Such is the financial landscape of the independent personal fanzine maker.

The world had not ended. I was still stunned by this, and unsure of what to do with myself. These were the strangely placid months between the Y2K computer meltdown and the September 11th attacks. My business at the bookstore transacted, I meandered pleasantly among the shelves for a while, but a grim reality was slowly setting in. Despite my best efforts, the adult future was beginning to loom. I announced to no one in particular: "Well, that's it. I've procrastinated as long as I could. Time to face up to the facts—I need to start looking for a job."

"A job?" the manager said, looking up from behind a stack of comics. "Well, actually, we're hiring."

What could I do? How could I communicate to her the magnitude of mistake she was about to make? There I was, the living embodiment of vocational inefficiency, a worker of such stunning powers of negligence and ineptitude that I had acted as a living pox on most every businesses I had ever worked for, driving them into the ground from the lowest rungs of the chain. I had proven a fatal Achilles' heel at the South Square Mall Cinema, Frickadill's restaurant, and even the beloved Chapel Hill/Carrboro Copytron, all of whom had fallen like flimsy card houses before the might of my all-powerful, destabilizing entropic life force. But I knew this place probably wouldn't check my references, and, even if they did, the series of "I'm sorry, this number is no longer in service" messages they'd encounter wouldn't be enough to tip them off. Even worse, I knew that my resumé was actually going to look good to them. For once in my life, I could offer my true curriculum vitae to a prospective employer. I could talk about my actual interests. I could look them in the eye and tell them about the zines, the comic books, the bands. Rather than eliminating me from consideration, this stuff was actually going to get me hired.

I got the job, and I had the band, and my next stroke of fortune was getting a gig as a columnist for *Punk Planet* magazine. If the name of the magazine sounds odd, one must keep in mind the context of the times, that there was a subcultural battle going on, a struggle to define (or definitively re-define) what it meant to be "punk." Of course, people had been claiming that punk was dead since about 1977, but somehow it wasn't; somehow it kept permutating itself, creating new variations on the theme; the implicit invitation of the genre—"you can do this too"—kept being accepted and acted upon. People kept forming bands; scenes appeared in the unlikeliest of places all over the world. The venerable *Maximumrocknroll (MRR)* magazine began publication in 1982, documenting this burgeoning worldwide phenomenon in the minutest of detail. *MRR* was widely regarded as the de facto "paper of record" or "Bible of Punk." In the early 90's, when the punk idea experienced a sudden moment of commercial success with grunge and Green Day, *MRR* retreated from the mainstream, tightening the reins on what they would cover to a very strict three-chord interpretation: pop, metal, post-hardcore, and emo were all disqualified. And yet the DIY spirit had broken out from the underground. Everyone wanted to do it. The scene was growing too diverse for one scripture.

Chicago-based *Punk Planet* magazine started publication in 1994, with a (literally) less black and white approach, and a different emphasis of coverage that included folk, country, indie-rock, hip hop, activism, visual arts, film and other media. The design aesthetic challenged the traditional scrappy appearance of zines with its perfect binding, pastel colors, and slick professional-seeming graphic sensibility. Some complained that it looked more like a coffee table magazine than a punk zine, and in truth when *Punk Planet* eventually appeared on the shelves at Whole Foods or Borders it didn't look all that out of place. In 2000, when I started writing a column, I told a friend the news and she scoffed and said, "Oh yeah, isn't that the magazine for people with office jobs trying to justify how they're still punk?"

Punk was experiencing an identity crisis, and I'd like to think I fit in well to this milieu. Reporting from the front desk at the bookstore or from the back seat of the band van, I spent the next years having what amounted to a public mental meltdown in serialized column form, editors Dan Sinker and Anne Elizabeth Moore patiently presiding over my tantrums as I wrung my hands and wrangled with the basic problem, the core question that *Punk Planet* seemed premised on, namely: how to apply the ideals of your youth to a world that is much more complex, much less black and white, than those ideals allow for? In other words: what if this *just goes on?*

•   •   •

I wrote for *HeartattaCk* magazine from Goleta CA, starting with an unsolicited article submitted in late 1999, wherein I urged readers to prepare for the very-soon-impending collapse of computer-based civilization. On the strength of those journalistic credentials, I was catapulted to columnist. Founded by Kent McClard, a former *Maximumrocknroll* contributor offended by that magazines' apparent attempt to put rules on what punk music could and could not be, *HeartattaCk* defined its parameters of coverage through the simple DIY litmus of refusing to review anything that had a UPC barcode on it. They had a reputation for being "politically correct," but in my experience the Goleta scene was a magical place, the people who worked on the magazine were smart, thoughtful and friendly, and looking back on it now, I realize that I devoted almost every column to trying to offend these nice people, to get kicked out, to go too far, write something out of bounds for a publication founded in a spirit of freedom of expression. Why did I do this? I don't know. I guess I was trying to the best of my interpretation to keep the flame burning, to rebel against whatever cards were dealt me, to be punk.

Towards the end of my stretch in Chicago I worked on a collective newspaper, *the Skeleton*, to which I contributed writing as well. There are some bits from that magazine in the final section of this book.

•   •   •

Quimby's outlived my employee curse, thankfully, and is still thriving. *HeartattaCk* and *Punk Planet* folded in 2006 and 2007 respectively, and I moved away from Chicago soon after that. My fellow columnists and co-workers have gone on to become novelists, journalists, editors, teachers, business owners, lawyers, and who knows what else. As for me, I vowed from the moment that I got that job at the bookstore that this was it, I had found my place, and I would never have another job while I lived in Chicago. Those were turbulent times, the early to mid thirties, transitioning into some form or iteration of adulthood, navigating the beginnings of that treacherous identity, with all its compromises, dark acceptances and uncontested contradictions. I went into it kicking and screaming, aware that all my dreams had come true and that once again the moral of the story was: watch out what you wish for. But in fact I never did have another job in Chicago, and arguably never really grew up either. I played music and wrote and drew comics. I scraped by and still do.

The world hasn't ended. I've lived outside the U.S. for about ten years now; when I read up on current events it is astounding, and when I'm back visiting, the tension in the air is palpable. How long before it all collapses? I remember this feeling: the vice-like grip of anxiety, the undercurrent of doom that is ever-present, driving you subtly insane. It's gotten bad; I don't know how you all are dealing with it. I carried these writings around for years, thinking that they were irrelevant, a relic of a gladly forgotten recent past—George Bush, the Gulf War, who wants to read about that? But perhaps apocalyptic tidings are now resonant again. The reason for writing it down, in any case, is to sketch the parameters of your experience, to find a greater thread, some kernel of truth and meaning, some reason that the machine of human machination functions the way it does. If nothing else, there is some comfort in comparison. The craziness of the present moment did not spring on us out of nowhere. Standing on the brink of destruction is not unusual; it is the perpetual state of things.

Punk is still around, and seems thankfully to be more diverse than ever. The hippies failed to levitate the Pentagon and quickly faded away; punk, with its more modest goals, has survived for forty years and taken root in soils as diverse as Soviet Russia and modern day Malaysia. It has rarely failed to levitate my spirits, and it is still here, even now, happening.

—Al Burian
Berlin, 2018

PART
ONE

ILL-FITTING SUPERHERO OUTFIT

Writing and Drawing for PUNK PLANET MAGAZINE

ILL OUTFITS

I knew a man who handled the problem of dressing himself in the following manner: he'd wear his clothes for two weeks straight, then go to a thrift store in whatever town he was in and buy the cheapest replacements he could find for every item he was wearing. He'd spend, on average, about five dollars, and he'd look hideous, clownish, outrageous sometimes. At other times he would actually pull off a pretty good outfit. Either way, two weeks later the clothes would be dirty and wrinkled, and then he'd trade them in for another set. The five dollars always seemed like a worthwhile investment on the day when he'd appear shiny and new.

I liked the idea: assuming that the thrift store would take his old outfits and wash and re-sell them, the resultant system was a de facto clothes library. Or, more accurately, you could say he was renting instead of owning. $2.50 a week is, if you think about it, not a bad rate for an unlimited and ever-changing wardrobe selection. But it was the selection which plagued him: never knowing what he'd look like next, a septuagenarian NRA member or a nu-metal acid casualty. This was a nerve-wracking uncertainty, and all that variance wore him down. He would describe his dream world, a utopia where everyone wore the same interchangeable navy-blue outfits, made from coarse, durable fiber. In this utopia people would exchange their pants and shirts with an identical set of pants and shirts every two weeks. The concept of ownership and social caste would be entirely removed from this clothing equation; we'd all relate to one another as equals, and I'd realize as he was describing it that these were the harsh dormitory lighting conditions of Eastern Bloc communism. I'd wonder if all utopias must, by necessity, include this monotonous wardrobe, if freedom always comes at the price of drab interchangeability.

People are always talking about how great it is to own things, but that doesn't make much sense to me. You're getting scammed paying rent, they say, when you could be putting that money into a mortgage and end up owning the place. Ownership is always assumed to be the fairer, more humane option, the natural state of things, although to me the natural state of things seems much closer to rental. Ownership just seems like a month-to-month agreement with a more celestial landlord, and when the hands of fate decree that the washer and dryer you've just paid off should now explode and fill the basement you own with scalding, soapy sludge, it's time to pay rent to the forces of entropy. Ownership is an illusion against death: I'm wearing my favorite shirt right now, and the act of wearing it is crushing me because I know that every second I wear it, I am wearing it away, and one day closer to wearing it out. This is heartbreaking, unbearable, and it is the pain of attachment which will bind me to it until it's worn away, until I have destroyed it—knowing the whole time that I should take it off, right now, and go down to the thrift store to trade it in for whatever I can get.

DecMber 27th, 1999. It's four days until the end of the world. You read the papers, and it's like the Book of Revelations. An anxious time. Palestinian hijackers hold an airplane full of people hostage in Afghanistan. Industries prepare for the worst. People plan parties or make meticulous, elaborate plans to avoid parties. The pyramids in Egypt will be bathed in light, holographic projections dancing across their huge, ancient surfaces as the artist formerly known as Prince performs his hit song "1999" below, to great applause and jubilation. Terrorist attacks seem inevitable; every day a new pick-up truck full of Anthrax virus is discovered in New York City or intercepted at the U.S. border, coming in from Winnipeg, Manitoba, transported by angry young ideologues with solemn, purposeful expressions on their faces and dynamite strapped to their bodies.

I've been trying to find a copy of the *New York Times*. All I have on me is a month old *New Yorker*. It's got good cartoons—despite my attempts at casting off bourgeois ideology I still find that shit pretty funny—but it's not quite the topical ointment of daily upheaval and prophecy fulfillment I seek, not part of the increasing hyper-speed race to the finish line.

I'm down in Florida to play some final shows before the end of the world. Florida is always weird and always a good place to go to accentuate feelings of impending apocalypse. We drive overnight and arrive in Jacksonville at 7:30 in the morning, then sleep in the parking lot of a Dunkin' Donuts. I wake up around one in the afternoon and take a walk across the tarmac tundra. Warm; the sky is the same color as the pavement. Cars hiss by, hermetically sealed against me and the outside. Standing in the space between a gas station and a fast food restaurant, along the burned-white dead shrubby grass that wheedles up against the highway, you get this acute sense of not belonging, out here in the air, breathing in the exhaust, the colorless sun irradiating you from above. Still, I've been in worse parking lots. This one's not so bad. It's astounding, really, how sensitized you can get to the differences between dead spaces, between varying tracts of stony sterile earth, glowing pale and moribund with neon and phosphorous.

Jacksonville has a reasonable downtown, a pretty good record store, lots of antique stores. A kid named Andy recognizes us as an out-of-town band and offers us free immunodeficiency smoothies at his place of employ, a smoothie shop. I've never had a smoothie before. It turns out to be pretty good.

The Red Scare has cancelled. We play in a seedy bar with Fin Fang Foom; Jacksonville is their hometown. There are a lot of people there to see them. It's always interesting to watch people you know interact with the people they know in their home town, without knowing the context, just imagining all the potential webs and social diagrams. I watch Fin Fang Foom converse awkwardly with people and imagine: ex-girlfriend, high school buddy, former arch-nemesis turned innocuous by time and distance? Who knows.

Yes—it might be unfair to feel that you can look at most people and pigeon-hole them immediately; I'm sure they are fascinating individuals with deeply unique personal histories and interests, and I'm sure I could learn a lot from anyone of them here, were I to spend enough time with them, which I'm not going to. In this more detached, temporary, and impersonal situation, it's easier to think sociologically, grouping people into aggregates. Superchunk T-shirt and short hair and glasses: he will look at the girl with the blond hair and thrift store dress across the bar, twice, then go and make conversation. Sit and watch. See? Like clockwork.

An older woman in a sort of black smock-like garment with huge, puffy moons and planets in soothing pastel shades all over it approaches me. She has the dazed, slightly pained expression of someone who's just been punched in the face. She asks me if I'm in a band. When I answer yes she begins lobbying me to let her son "jam" with us tonight.

"He's a musical genius," she insists.

"We're probably not up to his standards then," I say.

"He's like Eddie Van Halen," she assures me, repeatedly. "He's a prodigy. Please, sir, just give my boy a chance."

"Ummm, I don't know," I shrug.

"He won't leave the house," she pleads. "He just sits and plays the guitar all day. I keep signing him up for open mic nights and talent shows, but he won't leave the house. Please, mister. He's here tonight. Just give him a chance." She has a strange slurrrrrr to her speech, which seems to indicate that she's not just drunk but something a little more profound; perhaps she's on antipsychotic medication which isn't supposed to be mixed with the five or six beers she's had. She sways gently on her feet, her bulky frame shifting beneath the psychedelic poncho.

"Uh, well, maybe," I say uncertainly.

"If you want him to play, just say 'Billy, come up here to the stage,' during your set," she advises and shambles back towards the bar.

I walk over to my bandmates and give them the good news. "If we really fuck up a song or if everyone hates us," I report, "all we have to say is 'Billy, come up to the stage,' and this musical genius will come bail us out." We agree on this as the ejector-seat plan.

After we play (sans ejector), I sit down at the bar. I realize I have taken a seat next to the prodigy's mom when she taps me on the shoulder.

"This seat is taken," she says, indicating the barstool I've just seated myself on.

"Oh, sorry," I say, actually grateful for the opportunity to beat a hasty retreat, and start to get up.

"But you can stay until my son comes back," she grins, a drunken grimace, wrapping her arms lewdly around me, pushing me back into the seat. She leans forward and inserts her tongue in my ear. I'm too stunned to move. This woman is probably about my mom's age, but unlike my mom she seems to have a working knowledge of wrestling holds and quickly has my arms pinned in place. The next band has started. I can't hear what she's muttering now, but I gather from the undulations and quantity of foam at the corners of her mouth that it involves some obscene innuendo.

"Sure, just as soon as I get back from, uh, some stuff I need to do over by the other side of the room," I reply cheerfully, mustering all my strength to unpry her limbs' strangulating grip and bolt out of my seat. I'm not sure if I am actually going to make a run for it or am intending to just saunter casually away, but the decision is wrested from me, in any case, because as I turn to beat my retreat I find myself standing face to barrel-chest with an enormous hulk of a man, whose eyes, situated between well-kempt ponytail and neatly ironed Hawaiian shirt, burn with an unholy prodigious fire.

"Billy!" coos his mom gleefully. He stares at me, silently assessing. So this is Billy, the ejector seat, here to eject me from my seat.

"I hear you can play guitar like Eddie Van Halen," I say.

Billy shrugs. "I can play his shit," he says.

"He won't leave the house," his mom laments. "I keep signing him up for talent shows, but he won't leave the house." She sighs deeply, inflating the black tent she's draped in. "Oh, Billy, Billy, Billy," she laments in a high-pitched coo as she surreptitiously grabs my rear.

I try to make whatever conversation seems socially required for the sake of cordiality, wondering as I do why I'm clinging to these completely exploded norms of civility and conversational etiquette in the face of insane people, a woman in the throes of psycho-pharmaceutical bad reactions and her autistic son; with the clock over the bar glowing redly, one A.M., indicating the beginning of the third-to-last day before the world's end.

Billy's initial hulking menace fades quickly, and I realize he isn't going to beat me up for taking his seat and getting his mom all foamy-mouthed; in fact he doesn't seem interested in talking to me at all, particularly. He nods, goes "uh-huh," at the appropriate moments, but his eyes keep veering away—this must be a lot of sensory stimulation for him, depending on how exciting the posters and black lights back in his room are—his gaze following the trajectory of bodies as they circle and navigate the room, his face slacking in undisguised longing, as if those trajectories and sways are hypnotizing him, causing him to sway in accordance ever so slightly on his feet. His mom is totally tuned in to this, and every time his eyes veer away she takes the opportunity afforded by his distraction to whisper suggestively in my ear. Spittle-y lips seem to be a family trait, passed on through the DNA like male pattern baldness or schizophrenia. I give up on niceties, embrace the end times, and walk away to the other side of the bar, where I hide under a pinball machine for the duration of the evening, cowering and wishing someone would get me that *New Yorker* from the van.

END TIMES, CHICAGO

I t's nice to be able to listen to the national news and hear what the weather is going to be like tomorrow in your town. The forecasts call for these bizarre European temperatures, numbers like negative sixteen which I know cannot occur in America because then all motion would cease even on a molecular level and the universe would implode. Getting up most days around three in the afternoon, I catch on average an hour of sunlight, spending the dark hours tuned into NPR, huddling in the kitchen, drinking coffee, and listening to Midwestern blizzard reports, the white clouds of doom headed towards Chicago, which then segue into the even colder and darker world of U.S. national politics at the closing of the year 2000.

Today, as a foot of snow descends on Western Avenue, the frat boy son of one of the most unspectacular presidents in American history is declared the new person authorized to instigate nuclear holocaust if he so chooses. The pivotal supreme court decision seems to hinge (and I've only been following the whole thing with half an ear as I make the coffee) on it being somehow too complicated to actually count the votes cast by the electorate to determine whether said frat boy should rightly be in that position. Even George W. Bush's handlers admit that he was a C student, explaining that "C is the average. The American people want an average guy, someone who understands their needs and concerns, not some intellectual egghead. Most Americans get C's. It's the statistical average grade." I can dig that. Plus, it being, like, too much of a hassle to count the votes is the kind of Supreme Court decision I'd probably make so I could adjourn and catch a matinee movie.

NPR, my only connection to the outside world (besides the *Chicago Tribune*, which arrives with an unsolicited clunk every morning on my doorstep even in weather conditions where dialing 911 gets you a recording that says "call back in spring"), continues with its early-afternoon apocalypse theme, reporting that people in Europe are worried about renewed outbreaks of "mad cow disease," an epidemic caused by feeding the brain stems of cows to cows. "Mad cow" is one of the general nutritional hazards of cannibalism, although the cows who are being forced to eat other cows aren't the ones complaining, it's the human beings doing the feeding who then freak out about their own folly and send out panicked AP wires which are turned into newsprint and clunked on my front door. Why not just feed the cows something besides the brain stems of their already killed brethren and avoid the coming apocalyptic plague? I picture an English farmer (who, in my mind's eye, I base on Nigel Tufnel in the film *Spinal Tap*), shrugging his shoulders, and saying "Yes, well, but, we've *always* just fed them the brain stems. It's so much easier that way, you know." Again, the answer seems to boil down to the strange lethargic malaise which has gripped the human soul: despite impending Armageddon, doing anything to alter the course of destruction would involve "too much hassle."

"Mad cow" evokes some pretty good end of the world imagery, but it can't beat the almost Biblical-sounding *Tribune* headline "Rivers of Blood Flow in Congo." I turn to the page where I am promised topographic maps of these rivers, but find, instead, in a bait-and-switch tactic typical of the paper, an interview with the Doobie Brothers. The Doobie Brothers are back on tour and surprised to find that, as their original fan base brings their kids and grandkids in increasing numbers, new forms of dance are being introduced at the Doobie concerts.

Chicago Tribune: Mosh pits?

DB: (laughs) Sort of a yuppie mosh pit. You know, "hey man, don't rumple my suit."

And political leaders in Zaire, meanwhile, urge Zairian schoolchildren to study the current U.S. election in order to understand the mechanics of fraudulent elections. Zaire! Talking that way about us! Why, that country is right up by the rivers of blood!

NPR, meanwhile, has finished up the demoralizing news segment and moved on to music. They are bringing me a story about a jazz musician who had a brain aneurysm and had all memory of how to play his instrument erased. "I'm talking, zip, baby," the NPR announcer explains, enamored of some kind of bebop poet affectation whose origins I am too culturally stunted to be able to decode (hence, my interest in getting more worldly by listening to NPR in the first place), "This cat was gone, man. He had to learn it all again from scratch. But," the announcer happily informs us before playing one of his newest recordings, "he's back up to speed." Wow. Now there is a piece of reportage which really inflames the imagination. Here is a man who, having doubtless spent years building a career on that most slender and tenuous of transactable commodities, musical ability, has to one day face beginning again from ground zero. Imagine this person deciding to re-learn his instrument, and think about what it says about his self-image, his fundamental conception of himself: does he recognize in himself an immutable quality, a genetic constant, some latent and abstract potential ability just waiting to be turned kinetic again? In other words, does this jazz musician see in himself the antithesis of George W. Bushism and millennial human malaise, not just a C average ability somehow thrust fleetingly into the limelight, but actual talent, ability, the potential of doing something A+?

One is moved to wonder. What would I do if a brain aneurysm erased all of my, ahem, talents? Assuming all my, well, you can't exactly call them marketable skills, so let's say abilities to do things which seem more legitimate to me in some way than selling insurance, were erased in a sudden aneurysmal episode—what would my reaction be? It's hard to imagine I'd have the fortitude of our jazz musician. I guess I'd go back and look at my pre-aneurysmal output and try to glean whether there was something there which seemed like better than C work, which indicated some level of talent or interesting things to say or something that seemed worth resuscitating.

However, it's doubtful that I would find such a kernel of validity in my doings, since my immediate gut reaction to the NPR story is "I should fake a brain aneurysm to get out of writing this column." There would be something poetic and appealing about the post-aneurysmal persona. I'd probably enjoy going to parties a lot more if I had that up my sleeve as a conversational device: "Yeah, you know, I used to do all this weird stuff, I wrote for magazines, played in bands, but one day I had a brain aneurysm and it all got erased. I looked into re-learning it all but I figured the whole thing was too much of a hassle. Now I'm making a good living selling insurance. Why, what do you do?" Who amongst you, dear readers, will step forward and proclaim for yourselves A+ status. I suppose I could be giving this jazz guy too much credit as well. It's equally possible that his whole thing is not a product of intense belief in his own worthiness, but rather ascribable to acclimation, that he had just gotten used to the lifestyle, the smoky clubs, the free drinks, the late-night hours, which peddling his tenuously teetering one-aneurysm-away-from-nothing talent provided him. Did the prospect of just shrugging his shoulders, chalking it up to fate and getting a day job seem in that context less appealing than learning to play an instrument again?

My upstairs neighbor is reading a book called *Jazz Masters of the 30's* by Rex Stuart. The book is actually a collection of columns Stuart had written in music magazines in the 1950's, mostly recollecting his experiences on the New York club circuit in the 1920's and 30's, and, as my neighbor noted, "he can actually write really well, which is surprising, since most musicians are terrible writers. Or at least," he quickly corrected himself, "most of the really great musicians from that time were. Now, I guess you've got lots of guys who, uh—"

"Kind of half-assedly write and half-assedly play music?" I offered.

"Yeah, pretty much," he agreed. "It's kind of depressing, huh? It seems people are so freaked out about being mediocre themselves these days that they demand total mediocrity out of all their musicians and writers. No one wants to see anything which they can't look at smugly and think 'I could do that.'"

Which summates, unfortunately, both the punk ethos and the appeal of Boyz II Men, and even more ominously, the argument for why this detestable frat boy is an acceptable choice for president. Humanity, what is going on? I can accept that things are going downhill because of malignant evil, but not just because of general laziness. Having the chromosomally deficient emperor's son as the new emperor is classic decline-of-the-Roman-empire stuff, but can we at least feed some Christians to the lions or something? Tepid mosh pits at Doobie Brothers concerts just does not suffice as the over-the-top orgy of cultural hedonism which historically accompanies the decline of empires. The news is grim: It's negative sixteen degrees today, and humanity is going out like a bad sitcom. No grand finale, no last-minute revelations and tying up of all the unrelated plotlines; just cancellation due to lack of interest.

I've been having recurring dreams about my teeth falling out. A common dream theme, I'm told, and one which psychoanalysts say is representative of deep unresolved issues from childhood. Jessica Hopper tells me that losing teeth in dreams represents fear of loss of control or fear of powerlessness; however, in my case I think it's more straightforward, actual anxiety about losing my teeth. I have not been to the dentist in nine years; the last time I went I had my wisdom teeth out, which rocked, as I stumbled into the waiting room and loudly proclaimed to all in attendance, blood dribbling from my gauze-puckered lips as I did so. Still, neither the kind dental staff nor the copious amounts of narcotic sedatives prescribed to me elicited a return visit. I have done the best I could to follow the DIY guides to oral hygiene occasionally printed in *Maximumrocknroll*, but the dental news has been growing grimmer, and two new pieces of oral innuendo which have come to my attention of late have been almost enough to cause me to throw in the towel and get wooden dentures, George Washington-style. #1 piece of information is that apparently fluoride is a carcinogen. Yes, friendly fluoride, number one ingredient in all non-twig-based toothpastes. It gives you oral cancer, which just makes me livid. Here I've been, regularly forgetting to brush my teeth over the last decade on three out of five evenings, running out of toothpaste and neglecting to replace the tube for month-long spans, all the while wracked with feelings of the deepest, most profound guilt and anxiety about my negligence, and now it comes to light that these lapses may in fact be my only hope of not having to have my jaw surgically removed one day. Had I been the diligent thrice-a-day brusher I'd always liked to idealize myself as being, I'd probably be dead now. All that anxiety for naught! You're doomed if you do, you're doomed if you don't. That is the way of modernity.

Will-to-live-crushing information bomb #2 is that flossing is, in fact, more important for maintaining healthy chompers than brushing is. People, why wasn't I informed of this until now? My oral hygiene regimen has always functioned under the premise that brushing is the seat belt and flossing is the auto-inflating steering column-mounted air-bag—A nice bonus feature if you have a sweet set of wheels, but the common man is surviving just fine in Honda civics with seat belts and no drink holders. Now it's come to light that all this time I should have been shirking on the brushing (which I have been doing, at least) because, in addition to lowering my chances of contracting cancer of the lips, this negligence could have cleared up time and energy for the plaque-fighting mainstay of flossing! I have been bamboozled, and now am haunted by prophetic dreams in which my teeth crumble from my spongy skull and clatter to the floor, and in which I am reduced to gumming cream of wheat and pureed banana paste.

As a result I've been flossing maniacally as of late, trying to make up for lost time, and have succeeded as of 11 AM this morning in making my dreams reality, dislodging a large chunk of tooth while engaged in a vigorous floss assault on my pearly whites. The tooth shrapnel floated in my mouth for a moment before I picked it off of my tongue, assuming it to be a dislodged bit of food particle. It looked like an Indian arrow-head, or a miniature shark's tooth, and even now, many hours later, I can feel the gaping gap in the side of the lower bottom front tooth, where this grainy bit was torn from, a small cavernous trench, perfect for hiding a cyanide pill or smuggling a small stash of plutonium.

There is no sensation quite like the vertiginous feeling of having a dreamscape suddenly leap across the boundary of subconsciousness and into the plane of harsh waking reality. There is a dislocation, a sudden dizziness. You feel the urge to pinch yourself, to reassure yourself that it's only a dream even as the cold tiles of the bathroom floor, the slight sting on the cheek of a fresh shave, and a million other minute sensations align to impress upon you that, no, this is no dream; this is reality. The teeth are falling from the head like withered autumn leaves. This turn of events is devastating, horrible, and, once recovered from the initial, reeling shock, I've found all of my dental hygiene efforts brought to a crashing halt. I know that it's only a matter of time before the rest of the teeth begin raining down from my sad grimacing face, and what then?

I've decided to spend the evening involved in a deep and robust depression session, but my self-pity is interrupted by a phone call from Jessica, who shares none of my sorrow and woe, and is, in fact, calling to invite me out to a party. It figures. This is the strange, paradoxical nature of my life in Chicago: the city offers only decay and despair, dilapidated infrastructure, and demolished, crumbling facades, with the dull rapport of gunshots and the sanity-shredding muzak of waiting on hold with the phone company as soundtrack. And then on the other hand, you can never fully embrace the apocalyptic conditions because there is always a party to go to, there is always one more collection of bright and beautiful youngsters to offset the doom. That's the nature of urbanity, I guess: we're drawn to the death, we look good against it, it offsets our vitality, our essential aliveness.

Against my better judgment, I agree to go. Before long, I find myself in a car full of people, going to a party on the south side of Chicago. As the car detours from one location to another, zigzagging across the vast and expansive wasteland en route to pick up hipster after hipster, each of whose buttocks knifes deeper and deeper into my legs as the hipsters pile in, clown-car-style, forming a gargantuan and horrific human pyramid atop my lap— claustrophobia sets in, panic feelings. "Where is this party?" I want to know. "Pilsen," says Jessica. I calculate the number of sharp and pointy butt-bones which might be awaiting a ride between here and there. Chicago is vast and sprawling; the distance from downtown to Pilsen is the equivalent of driving the length of several towns in North Carolina, like going from Durham to Greensboro, which no one would ever do except in case of nuclear evacuation or, in my case, once as a teen in order to attend a Judas Priest concert.

However, I get the sinking feeling that nothing quite as spectacular as that awaits me at the end of this journey. In fact the most likely terminus on this ride is paralysis from the waist down. "Whose party is this?" I demand. "What's the occasion?"

"We don't actually know the people having the party," the front-seat enclave admits. "We heard about it on make out club dot com."

"Stop the car," I say.

They drop me off downtown, near a blue line stop.

"Are you sure—?" ask the hipsters. "I'm fine," I say. "Really, I'll just take the train home. Or walk. Or something. I'd really rather. It's fine." I do my best to contain myself. Losing composure is not going to help the situation.

"Are you OK?" I am asked very sincerely. What can I say? That I am having a dental crisis and that the idea of a party themed around people's affinity for a website based on their obsession with each others' mouths brings my loss of control and powerlessness issues to the fore? "I just don't really feel like—I mean—I just want to go home," I mutter. It's a little awkward, and I feel bad being the despoiler of the gung-ho party atmosphere, but I need to get away. I can't go through with this.

They barrel off, in hot pursuit of some joie de vivre, and I am left to wander around downtown for a while. It is deserted, enshrouded in a light drizzle. The buildings are majestically lit, amazing. I wonder, why don't I come down here and walk around by myself all the time? But, of course, you can't plan something like that, you'd never do something so sane and pleasant of your own volition. Left to my own devices, I sit in my room and stare at the walls and obsess about my own unraveling. But here, suddenly, I'm plucked out and placed in the greater context of the epic, rotting mouth of Illinois, out in the drabness of the cold Chicago death-night, the magnificent mile, walking around the block in silence, checking out the desolate city at night.

In the blue line stop, underground, I wait for the train with a platform full of other people. On a billboard across the tracks, a woman leers at me lasciviously, mouth open invitingly, tongue distended as she licks her lips. Her gaze is carnal, totally make out club. A small blemish on her tongue is circled. "It's tiny now," the billboard cautions. "Don't let it grow into oral cancer."

When the train comes it is only two cars long, already packed full of people, and the waiting passengers on the platform herd forward, mechanically, pushing and thronging their way through the doors, cramming their elbows and asses into the compartments. I try to push forward too, feebly, but my heart is not in it, and I straggle at the back until the doors hiss shut, and I am left alone on the platform, defeated. The blue line train shudders and hisses forward, rumbles into the tunnel, and is engulfed in darkness. I can still see the gleaming red lights and the faces of the passengers, literally pressed up to the back window, squished into place. And then the train breaks down, the car stops with a metallic shudder, and sits inert, just inside the tunnel. I can still make out the expressions of the people inside, pressed against one another, poker-faced, all perfectly still, trapped in the train. What can they do? Panic? Express feelings of powerlessness? Lack of control? What's the point? I recognize in them that dull look of acceptance, the implicit understanding that there are higher forces at work here, forces bent on making every decision the wrong one, the same evil deities who pulled the bait and switch with the fluoride, returning now to ensure that the most eager to get on the train, the ones most in a hurry or most certain of their right to crowd out the less assertive and take their place in the human sardine can of mass transit, would make the WRONG decision, would be the ones who end up stuck in the tunnel, the ones who don't make it home after all. If I had been a little more pushy, a little more assertive about my destiny, I could have elbowed my way on, I would have triumphed and boarded the blue line, and my reward for diligent ass-kicking would have been to be stuck in a suffocating sarcophagus of carbon monoxide and body odors.

You can't win! How can I even contemplate going to the dentist? How can I even think about oral hygiene and health in a city like this? This is the city of death, where even the right move is the wrong move. Best just not to brush your teeth, best not to try too hard. You're doomed if you do, you're doomed if you don't. When every move is the wrong move, all you can do is relax and accept it, hoping that between the party you missed and the train you didn't catch, somewhere in there you'll catch a moment of reprieve, an unexpected and pleasant walk through the crumbling scenery, and you'll notice how beautiful it is.

AMERICAN CUISINE

O klahoma City. It's a little early to be up, but here I am out at a greasy Midwestern diner, sitting at a table with Jim, the promoter of last nights' show, who also graciously let us crash at his apartment. Now it's time to head out of town, but first: breakfast. The diner is the kind of place that serves what is known as "American cuisine," which is, of course, not a cuisine at all but merely means that cholesterol is involved. America, why must your name always be synonymous with death? "American cuisine" essentially means "imperialist cuisine" or, to be less heavy-handed about it, "the cuisine of a variety of cultures and peoples, breaded and dunked in a fry-daddy." An American restaurant, that is to say, a restaurant with a U.S. zip code, might be Thai, Mexican, Indian, Italian or any of a myriad of other options, but when an eating establishment labels itself "American food," what does that mean exactly?

Trains of thought such as these, especially early in the morning before the coffee starts kicking it to me, are my standard downfall, at least as far as diners are concerned, because the waitress is always there to take my order before I've even cracked the menu open, let alone come to any conclusions. Caught off-guard, I mumble, "Uh, oh... hold on..." and open the menu, which leers back at me with its elaborate and daunting maze of options. Really, should this be such an arduous task? It's not like the menu consists of Chinese characters; it's just American cuisine. The menus in establishments such as this don't differ all too much, the most significant variables being in the realm of whether home fries are going to be $1.25 or $1.75. It is unlikely that some new tantalizing vista of breakfast experience is going to be hidden in there, and I'd like to think I have enough experience with this general genre of place that I'd have some rough idea of what I want, some regular item or set of items which soothes and pacifies with its comfort and continuity, the culinary ideal of the fast food franchise, familiarity. (At a copy shop where I once worked, I made xeroxes of the McDonald's annual stockholders report. It was an interesting document in that it stated this philosophy explicitly as the corporate strategy of the chain: to produce, rather than individual excellence in the individual franchises, a standard of 100% consistent mediocrity, so that from Maine to Thailand to Poland a person would never experience the shock of the unexpected, but could instead count on the exact same comfortingly mediocre item, the same ratios of special sauce, the same size patty, the same number of sesame seeds on the bun, etc). But here, in the greasy Midwestern diner, I do not have an airtight breakfast blueprint in place, and the devil is in the details, those oh so human errors and deviations which make greasy diners unique—will the home fries be overdone? How big are the pancakes? Do they or do they not come with toast? Do you have the green kind of tabasco sauce? Oh, God, condiments—what kind of condiments are available? How can anything be decided in relation to the purchase of potato products without full disclosure of all available condiments? The mind reels, panic sets in, I am paralyzed, my eyes locked in focus a few inches in front of the daunting menu, which floats in front of me, a menacing blur, as the waitress taps her pen impatiently against the small notepad on which she waits to scribble down my order.

"I'll have a hamburger," says Jim.

Eyes refocus on the omelette section. An omelette? When was the last time I had an omelette? Perhaps I would like an omelette, I think to myself. "Uh.... an.... omelette?" I stammer, uncertain, regretting the decision even as I articulate it, but knowing, already, that it's too late to turn back. Causing this poor waitress any more aggravation and corollary incentive to overlook our table on her coffee refill rounds seems extremely foolhardy.

"What kind of omelette?" the waitress wants to know.

"Try the avocado omelette," Jim suggests. "It's good."

"Avocado omelette?" I shudder. "Are you crazy? An omelette is bad enough. Avocados are entirely composed of fat. That's like getting a ball of fat in a cholesterol sandwich."

"What kind of cheese do you want in that omelette?" the waitress demands, on thematic cue.

"Cheese," I mutter. "A ball of fat in a cholesterol sandwich with cheese, fried on a lard-encrusted griddle. Um, listen, can I change my order to toast?"

Jim is laughing as the waitress shuffles away. "I guess you're watching your figure," he says.

"It's not so much about watching your figure as it is about not having a heart attack," I explain.

"Whatever," he shrugs.

"Jim, don't you ever worry about your health? Doesn't it ever occur to you to fret about how you're treating your body?"

"You're the one who's going to have a heart attack, not me," Jim says, "You've drunk thirty or forty cups of coffee and now you've worked yourself into a panic attack about what to order for breakfast."

Perhaps a valid point. My pulse is racing. "Fuck that!" I hiss. "YOU'RE going to have a heart attack before I do for sure! You drink tons of coffee AND smoke insane amounts of marijuana, the worst possible combination! The caffeine speeds up your circulation and the dope constricts your arteries! I'm surprised your head hasn't popped off already."

"I feel mellow," Jim laughs. "Look at your twitching, neurotic ass."

"A hamburger, Jim! A hamburger! You are a mad-man! Get with the program! Hypochondria! Fear! Disease! Tumors! Death!"

America, your very name means death, your cuisine is death on a bun with lettuce and onions. When the hamburger shows up, Jim munches contentedly. I like Jim, but he's an American, his lifestyle is a death style, he's pretty intense in the hedonistic excess department, and lecturing him on cholesterol consumption seems as futile a task as telling Attila the Hun that he shouldn't wear those rabbit-fur hats because it's cruel to animals. "Seriously," I say, watching him maw down, "You're not twenty anymore, you should really think about—"

My diatribe interrupted by a nerve-wracking, hacking, phlegmatic explosion from Jim, a lung-ripping coughing fit which erupts from his scorched and charred throat every few minutes, reminding me grimly that the cholesterol in the omelettes is low on his personal totem pole of inevitable deaths. Given the obviously adverse health effects of the astounding amount of pot he smokes, the best someone concerned about Jim's well-being can hope for is that he'll at least get some vitamin C from the occasional avocado. Cough brought under control, he chomps down on the burger, then chews reflectively.

"Let me tell you a something about death," he says. "Because I'm pretty sure I've thought about death a lot more than you have."

He takes another bite, chews, then says: "In the Gulf War, my job was to take land-mine sniffing dogs into previously carpet-bombed areas, to clear the way for advancing troops. A further duty of mine was to kill anyone I saw while searching through the rubble, anything living, be they soldier, civilian, wounded, woman, child, house pet. It's hard for me to explain what it was like. The carnage. The main thing which stuck with me was the smell. For years, I couldn't eat meat. I'd go to a cookout or something, and the smell of cooking meat would remind me of the smell of dead, cooked humans. I'd fucking freak out, start crying…."

"Woah," I say, "that's pretty heavy."

"Uh-huh." He takes another bite of burger.

"So… did you, uh, did you kill a lot of people?"

He shrugs. "I had been trained to kill, but when it came down to really doing it, I couldn't. So I refused and was thrown into military prison. The majority of the inmates in the prison had been put away, not for refusing to fight, but for excessive brutality, for being overly zealous in their application of violence—" what sort of activities qualify as immorally violent by the standards of the U.S. military I can scarcely imagine, but in any case—"The first night," Jim tells me, "this huge guy just flat out told me he was going to rape me as soon as the lights went out. What could I do? I went back to my cell and just sat there waiting for him. I sat there for hours, scraping my toothbrush on the cell floor, sharpening it into a point, just waiting. When the lights went out he came into my cell as promised; I was sitting down and he walked up to me without a word, dropped his pants and put his dick in my face, and I stabbed him in the leg as hard as I could with the toothbrush. I hit an artery. He bled like crazy. That got me put in solitary. I stayed in there a while, and when they finally let me out I punched the first guy I saw in the face and got put right back in. I preferred it in there."

Jim now runs the only hip record store in town, listens to a lot of metal, medicates himself with mass amounts of marijuana, and overall seems to be relatively sedate, stable, and, yes, happy. "Yeah, I'm thirty-five," he says. "But I'm happy right now. Frankly, I don't really care if I live to be fifty. Right now I'm happier than I've ever been in my life. I thought at thirty-five I'd be burnt-out, over the hill, miserable and waiting to die. But here I am, and for the first time in my life, I'm kind of content. I go whole days and feel good about myself and about my life. You know, honestly, I didn't think I'd ever feel this way. It's such a luxury, I don't want to give it up, whatever it takes—it was just so hard to get to this point."

America, your cuisine is listed in the intergalactic restaurant guides as the cuisine of darkness; the fatty, sleepy opiate of self-obliteration and hidden history. How does one approach a life story like that and make cutting your cholesterol a relevant and important topic? Yes, it makes sense to avoid the omelette as it makes sense, in its own way, to avoid all the vices because they are all vices for a reason, and when the teeth start to rattle in the skull and the sudden sharp pains in the lower abdomen become consistent and clearly tumorous in origin, in the psychic sonogram outline of pain you realize that, yes, every cigarette really did take seven minutes off of your life, and, yes, every omelette really did do its part towards clogging your arteries in some infinitesimal and immeasurable way; immeasurable, that is, until the day the blood backs up like rush-hour congestion in your veins and the heart rattles to a stop and the measure and finiteness presents itself, maps out the units of infinity calculation in one broad and overarching axiom statement: "Fuck, I shouldn't have eaten all those omelettes."

But shouldn't you have? When Jim talks about walking through towns littered with charred corpses, and how for years after the smell of cooking meat gave him post-traumatic panic attacks, is it then appropriate for me to tell him not to order a hamburger now? Is the hamburger his symbol of normality, of psychic healing, of being able to function like a normal person, an average American, even if it requires copious amounts of drugs to do it?

American cuisine! It makes sense. The country that would enact mass extermination abroad to preserve the inalienable right to cruise around town in big gas guzzlers on a Friday night must have the complementary meal plan, mass suicide and narcotization so as to forget, even for a moment, where we are and what we're doing. The chain-smoked joints exist below the surface; not on the menu, they're just as American as anything else, the Valium prescription or a few drinks after work or a hot fudge sundae—whatever it takes to pacify. Is it worth contracting lung cancer if the smoking which is going to give you the lung cancer is also the thing which allows you to get through the day feeling OK, even in the face of war and death, the lowest and cruelest brutalities of humanity? Is it better to get on some addictive state-sanctioned mind-altering medication, like Paxil, the drug which I watched my next-door neighbor in North Carolina get hooked on because he drank too much, only to find later that trying to go off it gave him seizures? The better it feels, the worse for you it seems to be. All we crave is escape, a moment of happiness. There seems to be no way there that doesn't kill us in the end.

I flag down the waitress. "More coffee," she predicts.

"Yes," I say, "and an omelette."

NO DOUBT

Despite her oversized coat and identity-obscuring hat, I recognize the singer of No Doubt immediately, checking in on British Airways Flight 112, London-bound, one person ahead of me at JFK airport. Her name is Gwen Stefani; I realize that I know this piece of information without knowing exactly how I know it. It's a mildly oppressive sensation: the realization that someone is taking up space in your head without offering you any in theirs. "You should be paying rent in my mind," one wants to sing, Guy Picciotto-style, at these moments. But my ire fades quickly, despite being rekindled briefly by the recognition, scant moments later, that her equally camoed companion is the lead-singer of Bush (that guy *really* owes me some rent; he doesn't take up much space but then again he is, as my own current landlord put it, "not a desirable tenant."). This man, Gavin Rossdale, is wearing a heavy coat and raver-type toque which he has pulled almost over his eyes—he is also wearing, I note, camouflage pattern converse sneakers meant to indicate I-am-a-famous-person-camouflaging-myself-as-a-commoner-as-evidenced-metaphorically-through-my-hide-in-the-foliage-themed-footwear. In any case, rather than the rub of celebrity-induced existential aggravation, the appearance of these two celebs fills me with glee. Although their presence on this flight does not, in and of itself, lessen the statistical probability of a hijacking, it makes the possibility of a hijacking much more exciting and entertaining-seeming. Given the passenger options, how likely is it that I'll end up the hostage?

There is a certain strange satisfaction in the thought that these people, who have handlers and managers and personal assistants, have been placed aboard my flight. It seems likely, after all, that someone somewhere has done some research into it and ascertained that this is a relatively safe-ish flight as flights go, and if the risks involved seemed minimal enough to allow these two alpha-people aboard, then I'm looking good. Someone must have done some research and even a minor, cursory inquiry into safety records, hi-jack preparedness, or weekends of the year when pilots tend to be most disgruntled would beat out my haphazard and hungover method of ticket purchase, the exact specifics of which presently escape me, though I do recall that it involved an 800 number which spelled out something along the lines of C-H-E-A-P-S-E-A-T. Funny, in fact, isn't it, that I cannot recall the exact 800 number, although this is a piece of information which might actually be potentially useful to know at some point in the future, whereas the name Gwen Stefani will only be useful in that I can say that I saw Gwen Stefani. And yet, there are those names, Stefani and Rossdale, cemented into the subconscious, never to benefit me again in any real way, crowding out space which could be storing phone numbers, my legal rights, the Pythagorean theorem. This is a depressing reality of the modern mind: like Geraldo Rivera opening Al Capone's vault, there is a lot of peripheral hype, empty hopes, and celebrity cameos, but inside the treasure chest itself we find very little of any substance stored. I listen to stories on NPR and five minutes later cannot recount them because I can't remember if it was Sri Lanka or Sierra Leone that they were talking about, but the first Duran Duran album contains Tel Aviv and the second one has Rio, and I will carry that information with me to the grave. Why the mind insists on being so lowest common denominator I do not know, but I hope that the other internal organs are not paying it too much heed or considering adopting the brains' lax work ethic—if my liver or pancreas decided to put in a 15-hour, hide-in-the-breakroom work week like my brain does, I'd be a dead man.

Then again, according to my more agoraphobic friends, I'm beating the odds as it is with my jet-setting lifestyle. Flight 112 will be my third international flight since Sept. 11 and I was on a plane and mashing the stewardess call button to demand another martini as early as Sept. 15, while my peers were still sending out emails announcing that henceforth they would not be leaving the house. Flying has become a dicey prospect in the post 9/11 era, or so one would be led to believe, despite the fact that terrorist commandeering remains statistically improbable. But, like the rare heart murmur which goes undetected until that first innocent snort of cocaine, it only takes one high-profile athlete's coronary to turn this possibility, slightly less common than spontaneous combustion though it is, into a national obsessive fear. The Society of the Spectacle, as Guy Dubord called it, needs its celebrities to guide us through the terrors of the modern age. Thus, HIV remained an obscure phenomenon in the eyes of the media until Magic Johnson introduced us to our first tragic celebrity case study. Similarly, Pamela Anderson, whose honeymoon home videos circulated VCRs across America, now bears the burden of introducing America to Hepatitis C, a common infection which you've been getting for years from that prep cook who didn't wash his hands, but which now, thanks to celebrity endorsement, is the hot new thing, this season's box office smash viral panic success story.

New terrors generate new celebrities. In *My People Shall Live: Autobiography of a Revolutionary*, Leila Khaled describes her experiences as an airline hijacker in the service of the Palestinian cause. Khaled is no Gwen Stefani, but in the world of international airline terrorism, she was perhaps the first high-profile media personality and reportedly a pretty stunning one at that: in "white bell-bottoms and a matching wide-brimmed hat," she waited to board a TWA Boeing 707 from Rome, flying to Tel Aviv, on August 29, 1969, hand-grenade in presumably matching purse, distracted from her terror mission only by what she calls "the human situation" of the Rome airport, i.e. Leila Khaled was just too damn good-looking to board a plane inconspicuously. A tactical error of the most basic sort: even I've spent enough time in the presence of Italian guys to know that you don't wear white bell-bottoms if you want to inconspicuously board and hijack a plane. Khaled describes trying to focus on her mission, on the plight of the

Palestinian children, on the book she's brought to read (*My Friend Che* by Ricardo Rojo, another accoutrement error), as a stream of men hit on her, making idle conversation, asking where she's from, where she's going, etc. "I had trained for every conceivable contingency," she relates. "I had mastered most operational details of the great Boeing 707." This "was something, however, I had not trained for.... I had to improvise and felt very uncomfortable."

In the end, Khaled successfully hijacked the plane, an act which generated enormous publicity for her cause and, subsequently, her. Khaled became, for a brief while, a terrorist celebrity, even having to undergo plastic surgery to disguise her widely-publicized good looks so as not to impede her next hijack attempt. In an interview with the German magazine *Spiegel*, the reporter seems noticeably awed, exclaiming, "Your beauty made a great impression on the world. Rumor has it that you underwent plastic surgery to change your facial features..... you sacrificed your beauty for the revolution?" Khaled is reported to laugh. "Everything is pretty much the way it was before," she assures him.

This is how history is written, in the names which become household, in the images which are repeated until their supposed moral becomes self-evident. The agents of terror have learned the rules of engagement long ago, had mastered the deadly art of the publicity stunt long before rock stars started overdosing to revive lagging record sales. We fear them because they pull us, the non-household names, into their web—so unlike our celebrities, who, Christ-like, assume the burden of martyrdom, the virally infected, cocaine-overdosed sins of the Society of the Spectacle. We remember the inconsequential periphera, the lyrics to heavy metal ballads from the high school dance, at the expense of another eradicated small section of our rationality: perhaps the one which stored some small bit of news, some information about Middle East politics, the history of terrorism, our civil rights.

Luggage successfully checked in and tickets assigned (I hope vainly that Gavin Rossdale will take a seat in first class while Gwen Stefani will be seated next to me in coach, a gesture of solidarity with the common folk, but have the sinking feeling that this is a fairly long shot), we traipse over to the security check area. As we walk through the glass gates and into the X-ray machine and metal detector area, I see the security guard look at the apparently average camouflage-converse-wearing everyman in front of me and double-take with that same jolt of reflexive brand recognition I felt at the ticket counter. I point at them and mouth the word "celebrities!" She smiles broadly, nods back at me, wide-eyed with enthusiasm, at the myth become incarnate before her. We put our hand luggage on the conveyor belt into the X-ray machine. Gwen and Gavin open briefcases and remove their iMac power-books. Another guard announces, "Alright! Could everyone please take off your hats and coats and place them on the conveyor belts." This is part of the new routine, anti-terrorist extra-security measures. The couple ahead look at each other, overcome with a slight but perceptible moment of frozen panic, then shrug it off, laugh. The jig is up. Underneath their heavy dull-brown everyman coats, they are wearing what might as well be superhero outfits, as if they may have to deboard the plane directly down steps leading onstage to an arena-rock concert. They whip off the jackets, and it's like floodlights go on in the security area, shimmery, glaring and brilliant, and the people in line shift and take steps back, then forward, not knowing what to do, dazzled—celebrities, ohh. Ahh. Bright red and blue, tailored and sequined, it's like American royalty, waving with that cupped hand Miss America wave, smiling phosphorescent, gleaming, dentured smiles, as if they've been suddenly teleported into the middle of this airport, materializing in the stead of those lumpy, ordinary sunglasses-and-hat-wearing Americans standing there moments before. A palpable feeling of euphoria overcomes the room. The passengers know, implicitly, that we are safe within those cupped hands. Nothing will happen. Civilization is intact. It's going to be OK.

I wake up on the morning of February 1, 2003, around noon, to the grim news that, for the second time this millennium, I have slept through a national disaster and will be condemned to experience it as an endless, all-day re-run. NPR loops the sound-bite proclamations of human tragedy, assurances that there was a "ninety percent probability" that the event was unrelated to terrorism, etc. I make some coffee, position myself in front of the radio, and set about the day's agenda of craft projects. This has become the daily routine of the chronically underemployed Burian: get up, listen to the news, wonder absently who I can borrow eleven bucks from in order to make rent.

Early 2003 is a desperate time, a historical impasse where only craft projects seem to matter anymore, a cultural moment where it becomes imperative to have it all on the sleeve, figuratively as well as literally. The NO WAR button on my jacket elicits random conversations with convenience store employees in my neighborhood. These conversations are statistically meaningless, but they make the people involved feel better. A good outfit or political slogan can do that.

"The bourgeoisie had better watch out for me," sang the Bad Brains, and it's true: the bourgeoisie ought to watch out for the punks of Chicago, they're looking great this winter. The punk aesthetic, i.e. "everything as obvious as possible all the time," is a look which hasn't felt this *tres chic* since the last time nuclear war got close enough to make writing "fuck the arms race" on your shirt with a sharpie seem the self-evident thing to do. But of course, punk fashion is like punk rock: punk tries to subvert rock but usually just ends up rock, and similarly, when punk meets fashion, fashion usually wins too—look at Elektroclash or the Sex Pistols.

However, despite its flaws, adherence to the punk aesthetic pays off for me on Feb 1, 2003, in that it positions me, world-historically, as a comedy innovator: not only the first person to make a joke about the space shuttle *Challenger* blowing up (11:58 AM, January 28th, 1986, at the Carolina Friends School, third period algebra, no one laughed) but also, now, the first person to make a joke about the crash-landing of the space shuttle *Columbia*, albeit this time in the form of sight gag / "wearable art." Before the coffee has even finished percolating, I've made a stencil echoing Jello Biafra's response to the *Challenger* disaster: *I'm glad the space shuttle blew up*. I ponder the implications of that slogan for a while, then get an old T-shirt out of my closet and stencil the message on to it.

It's not that I don't have sentimental attachments: at age ten I set my alarm for six in the morning to watch the televised takeoff of the first space shuttle flight. Swept up in the romance of space travel, I experienced a small moment of communal human triumph watching the launch, participating vicariously in history, in what Neil Armstrong called "a small step for man."

The romance of mass national feeling, however, was something I was growing uncomfortable with by the time I found myself in algebra class watching footage of a classroom full of children weeping for astronaut Christa McAuliffe, their exploded teacher. Perhaps my classmates were right to take offense at my yelling "hot for teacher!" during this replay. But now, with this new shuttle disaster, I feel vindicated: with two wrecks in 115 flights, the statistical probability of death by explosion for shuttle astronauts is about 1 in 57. This makes it seem less tragic and more the predictable results of engaging in an extremely dangerous and foolhardy activity. The odds for shuttle fatality are better than Russian roulette, yes, but much worse than for skydiving on crystal meth. Would the nation be morally obligated to mourn for victims of a government-subsidized program aimed at getting people to drag race gas tankers full of nitroglycerin?

The truth of the matter is I hadn't even known there was a space shuttle mission in progress, though in Israel (so the radio informs) it had been front-page news for weeks. Ilan Ramon, the first Israeli in space, is their Christa McAuliffe. The romance of mass national feeling: "It was a nice distraction from the Palestinian situation," Israelis interviewed on the radio admit. "It was nice to have good news for a change." Good news for a change! George Bush, only the day before promising war on Iraq in "weeks, not months," finds himself suddenly unable to openly advocate mass murder during the period of national mourning. The war will have to be pushed back a couple of weeks, but then it will be Valentine's day and that will be a PR nightmare too.

I would take all of this as a positive turn of events, if it weren't for people's general disturbing willingness to forget the public relations fiascos of the past, such as the harrowing admission by NASA scientists that waste plutonium had originally been slated to go into orbit as part of *Challenger's* cargo, meaning that the subsequent explosion would have led to cancer for somewhere between the population of Florida and the population of the world. Close call! But, using the laws of statistical probability, these same NASA scientists concluded that two in a row was really, really unlikely and sent the plutonium up with the next shuttle anyway. Hope there wasn't any plutonium on board *Columbia*—they probably wouldn't tell us if there was, but I guess we'll find out over the next ten to twenty years.

Come on, people: the space program is a waste of time and resources at best, an evil and immoral institution dedicated to mass annihilation at worst. It exists primarily as a research branch of the military-industrial complex, who are still hell-bent on Ronald Reagan's Alzheimer's-induced fantasy of "strategic defense" satellites to defend us against enemy missiles which exhaustive UN inspections have shown don't exist at a cost of billions to you, the taxpayer. Other than that, the space program is little more than a vanity project for mankind, who really wants to prove that we are not primates at all, but rather some sort of galaxy-hopping Marvel comics characters, while here on earth millions of humanoid primates starve to death.

I think a nation preparing to engage in the high-tech killing of thousands ought to spend a few days grieving for seven people who died for essentially no reason inside the most advanced piece of machinery on the planet. Ilan Ramon said that he hoped his voyage would be seen as symbolic; symbolism doesn't get much more heavy-handed than this. If I were the sort of fundamentalist nut-bar George W. Bush is, I'd be scared. On the eve of war, God's message would appear to be loud and clear: *I am not on your team, Judeo-Christians.* If I was that particular nut-bar, I might spend a little time thinking about what I've done to anger my deity at this point. I might try to atone for these errors before embarking on any further righteous crusades.

But people wear their hearts on their sleeves and sharpie their emotions onto T-shirts, not rational arguments. As it was in Greg Kohlbach's third period algebra, so will it be today. Nobody gets my jokes. My roommate sees the shirt, folded over a chair to dry.

"*I'm glad the space shuttle blew up*? That's fucked up," she says.

"What do you mean?" I say, "That's funny."

"You're fucked up," she says, shaking her head and walking out of the room. Unnerved, I call a few friends and run my idea past them. Opinion seems unanimous: it would be in bad taste for sure, and possibly dangerous, to wear the shirt out of the house. I get off the phone discouraged. Then it occurs to me that I should have asked one of those people if I could borrow eleven dollars.

USA AT WAR

The weather in Chicago has gotten back on its miserable early-spring track, after a seductive spell of balmy, cloudless mid-70's days, which happened to coincide with the beginning of the war on Iraq. These freak weather patterns no doubt sent this way by Allah to encourage protest and maximum occupancy downtown during anti-war marches. But now blonde-haired, monster truck driving Jesus is back at the helm, and icy torrents of polluted and just-over-freezing rain are gushing down, keeping people home.

Those early days of war were conflicting and emotionally divisive, a confusing set of mixed feelings, and perhaps the weather was the final insult, a taunting seasonal bait-and-switch which turned our moment of righteous anger into spring break '03. This seemed to offer conclusively that Jesus and Allah are both the fictitious delusions of deranged, fanatical imaginations, while the existence of ancient Greek style gods, with all the foibles and human fallibilities intact, seems confirmed. These are the types of Gods that might travel to earth in the form of a bull to get it on with Columbia college undergrads; such Gods would certainly enjoy taunting some of their earthbound wards in the form of inappropriately pleasant weather for angry demonstrating.

I run into my ex from North Carolina at one of these protests, and we walk along together for a while. I tell her I feel bad for the cops assigned to oversee the marches, lined along the street in their bulky riot gear. The weather is a balmy T-shirt temperature; it must be insanely uncomfortable in an umpire vest and motorcycle helmet. She's unsympathetic to their plight. "I can't stand it when the cops check me out," she says. I check the cops out, and, it's true, they're checking her out. But the cops are only human, and, in all fairness, everyone is checking out everybody. In a city whose climatic extremes kill people in both summer and winter, and where the transitional seasons last anywhere from four days to a week and a half, spring weather is precious, it unifies the population in a common human thaw.

The simultaneous advent of spring and aggressive preemptive warfare has made these great times to be a single left-winger in America. There are protests to go to, networks being networked, connections being made, common interests assessed. A lot of phone numbers are being exchanged. But, like the anti-war movement of the 1960's, you wonder if all that digit-swapping is going to add up to a solid, organized political force or just add up to another generation of children conceived while listening to Creedence Clearwater Revival.

•   •   •

If you think the current U.S. occupation of Iraq is bad, consider the Mongol hordes, who in the 12th Century ransacked and looted Baghdad with merciless ferocity, killing a million and a half people and destroying libraries full of ancient knowledge and philosophy, streams of human thought never again to be recovered. Shortly after the toppling of Saddam statues, there was some small outcry over the looting of the Iraqi national museums, but the reality of the situation is that those museums housed only the fragmentary remnants, the leftover debris of the much more thorough and far-reaching cultural annihilation enacted by the Mongols in the 1100's. The Mongols, like the Europeans at that time, were living in a dark age as far as literature was concerned. Illiterate, superstitious, and plague-infested, European people spent little time reading and the majority of their time burning people at the stake, gouging out eyeballs, and otherwise acting about how they always do. To the east, the Mongols had more advanced social organization and a blood thirst which makes even white people seem pacific. Baghdad has been cursed throughout history to be wedged in between these barbarian hordes. In 1100, the city was arguably the pinnacle of human civilization. They boasted literacy rates upwards of 90 percent, a flourishing book trade, and libraries filled with . . . well, thanks to the Mongols we will never know exactly what they were filled with, but considering that the ancient world gave us Sophocles, Confucius, and the Koran, and the modern world has given us Nietzsche, Ayn Rand and Howard Stern, it's hard to argue that the trend has been towards lucidity. I'm willing to bet there was some papyrus worth reading in those libraries, had it only survived the sacking.

But then again, when you start talking about "stuff worth reading," I begin to feel some affinity for the Mongol point of view. Even today, in the relative darkness of our current age, there is an overabundance of stuff worth reading, in fact there seems to be an insane excess. Ed Willmore loans me a copy of Natsume Soseki's *Kokoro*, which he tells me is "the novel you can't graduate high school in Japan without reading." This book sits on the shelf, making me a Japanese high school dropout at age 33. Shouldn't the vast oceans between us be preventing Soseki from getting on my shelf in the first place? Wouldn't reading some Haruki Murakami get me further, in terms of making conversation at parties? And what about Tony Lazzara's recent loan of *Lucifer Rising: Sin, Devil Worship, and Rock n' Roll,* which he assures me "has a great King Diamond interview?" How do you prioritize? Where do people find the time to read? I'm practically unemployed, and I spend little to no time keeping current on cinema and television. Still, I have difficulty scheduling reading time and, when I do, maintaining the focus necessary to absorb anything much more complex than the average Marvel comics storyline. Observing the behavior of our troops in Iraq through blurred video footage and anecdotal snippets that trickle back to us here, our place in history becomes depressingly obvious: we are not readers. In America, it is not encouraged or validated as a practice. And when our culture is exported abroad, by force or free markets, we look a lot like what we are: the latest wave of barbarians, ripping apart the fabric of civilization with the crude, contemptuous scimitar of the Mongols.

•   •   •

On the first really nice day of spring, I find myself walking around the Ukrainian village. I decide to stop in at the Communist bookstore to see what kind of books they have in there. The shelves are filled with weighty tomes and incendiary pamphlets, but like the libraries of Baghdad, these are works I will never get to peruse, because before I can make it to the shelf an overzealous Communist has already cornered me into one-way conversation. "Hello!" he says, and then as if speaking to a small child: "have you heard about the re-vo-lu-tion?" In fact, I have heard about it, and I have even read a little about it. My first year of college I went so far as to join a young Communist organization and attend their annual convention in Detroit, Michigan. Here, I learned that the organization was non-sectarian, allowing for any shade and nuance of ideology as long as it fell within the lines of Marxist-Leninist-Trotskyism. Similarly, I notice that this book store is decorated with posters of Marx, Lenin, Mao, and (most disconcerting) a framed oil-painting of RCP chairman Bob Avakian, even as the guy standing between me and the bookshelf explains that the RCP is also "non-sectarian." Come on, guy: even differentiating only between the most obvious sectarian lines, it's clear that Marx was probably a big reader, Lenin wrote a lot but wasn't a big reading advocate, and Mao was definitely more on the mass killing side than the reading side.

Looking around the dimly lit store, whose half-dozen inhabitants are huddled in the corner having a meeting about something, oblivious to the sun shining outside, I can't help but think that the Communist party isn't really how I like to party. I wonder: Am I an Anarchist? The question has been in the back of my mind, haunting me, for years, and I have put off seriously grappling with it because the prospect of adopting as a serious life philosophy something which I first heard about from the Sex Pistols—well, that doesn't exactly stamp me as a reader myself. To remedy this, I've been taking some tentative steps towards reading up on anarchist philosophical tenets, but have been frustrated to find that, as Daniel Guérin puts it: "It is difficult to trace the outlines of anarchism. Its master thinkers rarely condensed their ideas into systematic works. If, on occasion, they tried to do so, it was only in thin pamphlets designed for propaganda and popularization in which only fragments of their ideas can be observed." Then again, I guess you could argue that a philosophy that knows when not to write is perfect for a society that doesn't know how to read. Besides, aspirants to real human liberation would be in the park on a day like this. Thus endeth my affiliation with the Communist Party as I politely excuse myself and head back out into the sun.

•   •   •

Otherwise: war doesn't alter the quality of life in U.S.A. drastically. There are still column deadlines, although I feel now more justified than ever in blowing them off and drinking heavily instead. These are, after all, days of intense darkness, sun notwithstanding. The mild oh-fuck feeling of the 2000 electoral shenanigan was a shit-I-locked-my-keys-in-the-car type of creeping doom, but post September 11 America has developed a special, new kind of bleakness, something never before felt by me in my many years as a citizen particularly enamored of the American darkness genre.

I run into Tony Lazzara at a bar one night, belligerent, articulating the subconscious sentiments of the mass mind. "Fuck it, man," he says. "I'm ready for it. Bring on the End Times. Drop the fucking bombs on us! Bring it! I know how to skin an animal. I'm ready for that Road Warrior shit." You hear this sort of thing advanced as a line of argument for ordering another drink often enough these days, but for the sake of accuracy in belligerence I feel compelled to point out the logical flaw to him.

"There is no one who can drop bombs on us," I remind him. "We live in the most powerful country on earth. There is no apocalypse coming. No one is going to do anything to us in the immediate future. Over the rest of our lifetime, yes, there will probably be isolated acts of horrible recrimination, followed by increasing restriction on our civil liberties. But probably no apocalypse."

"Well, OK, Bring on SARS then," says Tony. "Whatever!"

Lazzara's pro-apocalypse stance may explain his lack of attendance at anti-war demonstrations—"bring it on, I know how to skin a squirrel" not being one of the favored chants of the modern American Left—or maybe it's just wishful thinking that reads a strain of nihilist rationality into his lack of engagement. How else is one to explain the noticeable lack of enthusiasm for social activism on the part of the born and bred Midwestern indie rockers compared to, say, southeastern transplants? Do southerners have a deeper sense of social injustice? Or do they just understand that you are supposed to go outside when the weather is nice? The American South has a long history of terrible social injustice, and by regional default these events have often coincided with great weather. Perhaps southerners are just more comfortable with that particular paradox.

COMICS AND REVIEWS

One week home between tours at the end of the summer, biking to the grocery store on the bicycle my boss at the bookstore traded me for a comic strip I'd drawn. A good trade for me, a few hours of not-so-hard labor, doing what I'd be doing anyway, at a better hourly rate. This bicycle, the most luxurious luxury item in my possession, purchased on the psychic credit of latent potential—Cisco, the neighborhood weed dealer, marvels: "Nice bike, Holmes! You need to start locking up that back wheel, though!"

Chicago in the summer is a different world than in the winter; it's an odd home base, a schizophrenic city, augmenting as it does the already schizophrenic feeling which the international-jet-setter-on-no-money-down-and-just-the-hope-that-my-doodles-will-be-worth-something-on-eBay-one-day lifestyle instills. In the grocery store checkout line, I see a booklet for sale on "what the Bible REALLY says about the end of the world," but it costs $1.19. My horoscope in a tube is only 35 cents. Should I base my theological paradigms on what sect offers the cheapest literature? "What the Bible REALLY says about the end of the world" is still going to beat out *Punk Planet* on a cost-to-Armageddon-oriented-revelations ratio, although judging by columnar responsiveness, it's not revelatory apocalypse warnings which y'all readers are seeking, it's comic strips. Who can blame you? Of all my efforts in these pages, some of which were written rather quickly and some of which were labored over at great length, the thing which has generated the most vociferous response has been the comics, knocked out in about 45 minutes under deadline pressure, justified tenuously along the thematic line of "art and design issue" and controversial, apparently not because of the form but because of content, mainly in that it made fun of people for using computers. I did not think of this as a particularly controversial standpoint to take, but armies of incensed graphic designers and otherwise "punk"-associated employees of the "computer world" have let me know otherwise, though sadly not in comics form.

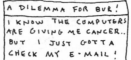

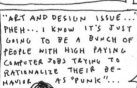

Meanwhile, the reviews have been pouring in, and they're not looking too good either. "This guy went from biting humor to simply biting," reads one review of a recent fanzine I've made. "At least sign to a corporate press, that way people who are trying to do something positive with their work can write you off as a sellout." Even *Punk Planet*—this very magazine!—won't give me a good review! "Self-indulgent blathering... Burian seems to need antidepressants lately," the reviewer scoffs. Antidepressants? What I need, people, is a healthy dose of nepotism. Looking over the list of reviewers, I see several people who should have been able to take care of this. Vincent Chung, where are you to give me some much needed nep? Brian Moss, you're always nice to my face, can't you do something for me behind the scenes?

Moreover, the whole premise of the "depressing" accusation really irks me. What's up, readers, are the pastel colors and tasteful fonts softening your brains? If this is the case, then my column ought to be the most popular item in the magazine, since my goal as a writer is almost exclusively to provide light comedy, a little soft-boiled ha-ha to counteract the mostly grim news from everywhere else. So either a) I'm communicating *the opposite* of what I'm trying to communicate—not a very good review of my writing abilities, b) you people just don't get my jokes, or c) what we have here is a failure to communicate, a lack of correlating givens. It wouldn't be the first time. The punk aesthetic—loud, obnoxious, confrontational, *real*—has never come naturally to me, but I've learned it, and I've been happy to parade it around at times, like an ill-fitting superhero outfit. A confrontational attitude seems to me a good way to face the daily tragedy head on, without buckling under the weight of it, a good way to laugh and thereby keep from crying. Of course, either reaction is perfectly appropriate. It's the non-reaction that bothers me, and your demands that I not broach the subjects, that I not display a reaction either. What's going on here? Perhaps it's you who ought to be taking a few less antidepressants?

THANKSGIVING

Let's celebrate our sorry lives
Quick little buzz could kill some time
Functioning's rough with shit on my mind
Gotta be blind for just a little while

A uthor of the above lyrics is Scott Hicks, friend of mine from the old days, a couple years younger than me and expecting his second child, cleanly shaven head, happily married. Homeowner, landlord (he owns a second house which he rents to a college sporting fraternity—"They're nice guys, when they don't party too much," he says), and the overlord of some domain on the internet, which provides him less of an income than domain-overlordship did in medieval times but enough to get by, apparently.

Sitting in Scott's living room in Greensboro, North Carolina, on a visit home, going down the list of people we know in common from our mutual past, checking them off one by one, where they are and what they're doing. We're two graphable blips within an aggregate, not the opposing poles of existence by any means but not living anything like the same life either. Our worldviews are still pretty similar, both to one anothers' and to our younger selves: we'd probably both still describe ourselves as punk. His wife, Gina, plays with the kid, Max, on the floor, half-listening to him and to us, smiling to herself. Everything in Scott's life strikes me as very *functional*: Gina and Scott are, in fact, one of two functional couples I know of currently in existence in the world. Four people out of seven billion involved in functional relating is not too bad, I guess—it confirms my general intuitive sense of the matter, which is that relational functionality is an attainable state, though statistically very improbable.

I will always think of Scott in terms of his Thanksgiving story, told to me in the parking lot of Revco in Durham, North Carolina, when he was about seventeen years old. Sitting on a curb in the fully-bloomed sketchiness of his youth, he had recounted the events of the family festivity which had occurred a few days prior. His grandfather, he said, had made a toast, addressing the individual men of the Hicks clan and, arriving at Scott, had noted that he was the last in line, "the last of the seed-bearing Hickses." Scott had repeated the phrase to me and laughed, grinning with a strange mixture of chagrin and pride as he described the ensuing uncomfortable silence in the room, all eyes turned towards him, brows furrowed in contemplation of him, the terminus point of the Hicks family lineage.

But here we are now, in the living room of his house: Scott Hicks, upstanding member of the community, responsible citizen, conscientious father. The Hicks line has successfully forged on, and without the sharp turn towards cannibalism and satanic idolatry which the family had darkly envisioned those many Thanksgivings ago.

Thinking about Scott, and where he is in his life right now, I have to wonder: Am I letting team Burian down? I try to keep the family up on my recent doings, I send home my press clippings and appearances in the police blotter. But is this enough? Am I adequately providing the antecedent generations with the only real thing they ask of you, the sigh of relief that comes with not turning out how you threatened to?

.   .   .

Woke up, I had the same clothes on I had on last night
Damn, I must have passed out
And cash is just like the clothes worn yesterday
I gotta get my ass out
'Cause I refuse to be a bum
Especially comin' where I'm from
I'm a provider

Narrator of the above is the protagonist of a song by the rap group N.E.R.D.; this is a song which I find myself musing on often, trying to deconstruct its themes and inflections, trying to understand its message, compare and contrast, and in that way somehow better understand my own position in the universe. Here is a song propelled by what heavily bearded German philosophers of previous centuries referred to as a dialectic, meaning a clash of fundamentally oppositional forces, whose clash, rather than being entirely destructive, becomes the engine which propels the actors forward. The central tension of the song is between the incongruity of its form—romantic slow jam—with content, which is the narrator's defense of his drug dealing. "I'm a *provider*, girl," he explains, his voice rising in pitch as he intones the phrase. He means to present his position as noble, romantic, and honorable, and in the same way that the lyrical content subverts the junior high school schmaltziness of the musical backdrop, the narrator's reversal of conventional morality challenges our notions of correct, responsible behavior. The irony that someone would engage in that most rhetorically anti-family of activities—drug dealing!—precisely out of commitment to supporting his own family, the anti-social action as an expression of adult social responsibility, comments interestingly both on the hypocrisy of middle-class "American dream" expectations, the impossibility of their fulfillment for the underclass within the current capitalist framework and the extent to which core patriarchal values of our society—commitment to the nuclear family and a success-model based on earning ability and "providership"—are embedded in even marginalized subcultures, which, on their surface, seem anti those values and expectations.

And, of course, a further irony is the commentary on myself vs. Scott Hicks, he in his own way attempting to synthesize the dialectically oppositional strands of sub-cultural affiliation with the realities of middle-class existence, fatherhood, fiscal responsibility, coming to some sort of synthesis, more or less, of "punk parenting," an idea which seems as incongruous a notion as the N.E.R.D. singer's sugar-coated coo that if he doesn't end up having to blast a state trooper with his shotgun, he can't wait to get home and hold your hand, girl. And then myself, dancing about in a room in Chicago, Illinois, where the walls are almost completely covered in garbage I have found and tacked up, the décor of a deranged twelve-year-old with obsessive-compulsive disorder, listening to the song and just laughing my fucking ass off because there is no way, really, that I can relate the sentiments of this song to myself. I might as well have phonetically memorized the Martian national anthem. I am in no way a provider to anyone, I am barely even capable of taking care of myself. The protagonist of the song is a graphable blip on a continuum with Scott Hicks, and it is a graph on which I do not register at all, on which I am statistically superfluous information.

·   ·   ·

Walking to the grocery store down a side street, I find myself behind a pack of kids, probably twelve or thirteen years old, all boys, sauntering down the street, dressed almost identically in baggy sweatpants, puffy hooded jackets, ski caps, the color scheme a uniform muted grey. I wonder if they met up on a corner somewhere earlier all dressed alike, spontaneously, somehow tapped into the thirteen year old fashion mass mind, or whether these tough little guys were on the phone with one another this morning, like adolescent girls, plotting today's outfits: "Yo, man, tell Terry he can't wear that puffy jacket with the green piping anymore. That's a fashion *faux pas*, mutha fucka!" The gang of junior high school hooligans struts along, passing as they do a solitary, similarly attired thirteen year old, albeit dressed in a monochrome of a more blueish hue. He cowers slightly, eyes fixed straight ahead, while they murmur icy and implicitly threatening what's ups to him. As he passes me, our eyes meet. I am impressed by his mustache. Pretty good for his age; he looks like a tiny adult, like a bonsai'd gangster. He sees me, eyes still locked in the cold poker face of fear, and then, registering me, smiles broadly, almost seems ready to burst out laughing. Perhaps, I think, it's the relief of seeing a mature, adult presence, and knowing that no harm can befall him? But, moments later, I notice one of the grey-uniformed miniature hoodlums turn around, spot me, make that "pfffhhh—" noise one commonly associates with the act of reflexively spitting out a beverage. He elbows his compatriots, who all turn around and check me. Their eyes light up; very soon they are openly laughing and shouting mocking epithets at me. Seeing as they consider the exact uniform they are wearing but in a slightly different chromatic shade worth an angry scowl, it makes sense, of course, that they find my outfit incalculable on their internal fashion richter scales, a disaster of such monumental and devastating magnitude that, like an earthquake which has not only killed your loved ones and destroyed your belongings, but has actually swallowed your entire country and obliterated all traces of anything that gives your life even abstract, symbolic meaning, there is nothing to do but get hysterical in the face of it, laugh your ass off.

I walk behind the kids, trying to catch the gist of their tittering, exuberant denunciations of my wardrobe. Finally, one of the boys, as if elected spokesman, turns around, and summates their critique in one word, yelled over his shoulder at me in the form of a schoolyard taunt. "Seventies!" he yells.

The kids slow down so that I am forced to pass them. This way they don't have to strain their necks during an inventory of my fashion offenses. They follow me down the street, laughing and yelling insults at me as if I'm an inanimate object, a trailer for a movie or a poster on a wall. This sort of thing happened to me when I was thirteen all the time, I recall. Being taunted by seventh graders no longer bothers me in my thirties. I congratulate myself on the victory. I actually savor the taunting, and I slow down to catch the specifics. They are discussing my pants.

"Nigger's wearing bell-bottoms!" gloats one.

That's startling. I've never been called a nigger before. I'd never expected to, honestly, being obviously caucasian. These thirteen year olds are either employing some super-advanced usage, or the word seems to have reached such lingual saturation as to have all meaning stripped away from it in their minds; it seems to simply mean "an annoying object in my way." This was Axl Rose's argument during the *Lies* era of Guns N' Roses, that the "niggers and po-lice" he sang about were figurative, merely metaphors for the daily hassles of life. No one bought his argument then, and I don't think we should fall for it now. But these are not my kids; it is not my responsibility to raise them, or even to question their conversation. I keep walking, and they soon grow bored of me and fall behind.

•   •   •

> *"I am punk because I simply feel there is something wrong with our society. It's not something I can argue, it's just a feeling"*

At a show at the Fireside Bowl, the day before Thanksgiving, I wander around staring at the people in attendance, awed and cowed. I'm out of fashion here as well, an anonymous anomaly once again, amongst the decked out and dressed up punks, who look about the same as they've looked since time immemorial, with the same bands written in marker on their jean jackets which I might have written on a jean jacket with a marker in some primeval time. Not many new names added to the canonized set of standard logos and slogans in the past decade, the Crass snake still consuming itself, the Dead Kennedys logo still spelling out "decay" in the phonetic language with which one reads personalized license plates. The hairstyles remain consistent, as well. A guy with a towering, primped mohawk talks on a cell phone, the scene thereby located within the space/time continuum as early twenty-first century, the hairstyle suddenly comically functional, useful for phoning in that it keeps his hair off his ears, as if the hairstyle was always intended to compliment cell-phone usage, as if the hair had been standing at attention for years, anticipating the gadgetry to come. Passing by me, Miles Raymer, 25, dressed in a too-tight yellow Circle Jerks T-shirt, his wild curly hair looking very seventies, says to me, "Man- when I was seventeen I never thought I'd feel this out of place in a room full of punks." I wander into the bathroom. Two white male suburban punks, about seventeen, in full gear, discuss a mutual friend: "Oh, yeah, Oz, man, he's my nigger, man!" says the one. The other kid nods, indicating that that's a perfectly acceptable description, and that he understands exactly what that entails and encompasses.

The "I am punk because" quote on the previous page is from the current issue of the German fanzine *Blurr*, which contains an interview with a group of young punk teenagers from Düsseldorf, Germany. One of these kids, Mici, is pictured with an astounding, Thanksgiving-turkey-like plumage, multi-colored and standing straight up. His hair is not so unlike Scott Hicks' civilization-derailing mane of the Revco parking lot. Underneath this astounding display, the face of a cherub, a doughy innocence and unconcealable wide eyes. He's been punk for about a year. The interviewer questions him regarding his motivations, here in the twenty-first century, for carrying the banner, for refusing to let the lineage die. Mici explains: "I started to get interested in left wing theory at fourteen. I was reading Marx and stuff like that, then at fifteen I had had enough theory. I wanted action. Being a punk came not so much from a musical connection, it was the appearance, which shows radicalism and an opposition to this fucking world, this bullshit culture. That's why I thought, I'll get a mohawk."

This kid, in Düsseldorf, Germany, not so unlike me, a victim of irrational sentiments and inarguable convictions. And we have other things in common, too: our appearance shocks the populace, induces mockery and ridicule. Be careful what you wish for, I'd like to tell Mici.

.   .   .

Let's celebrate our sorry lives, says Scott. Thanksgiving has been a much better holiday in my personal roster since I stopped spending it with family and started spending it with friends. Nothing against the family, but familial obligation is an obligation by definition, a form of social pressure which only that unit can generate. Friends are the people you choose to have around you because you enjoy their company, and if you have some, that's worth celebrating.

I spend Thanksgiving at Roby's house, my annual tradition, thinking about Scott's story. Several people tell me their own Thanksgiving anecdotes: Nandini tells me about leaving work two years ago, her last words to her boss being, "Watch out for that tryptophan coma," in reference to the sleepy state eating turkey would induce, not the actual coma her boss would slip into over the holiday weekend, never to wake again. Cynthia tells about working at Darryl's restaurant in Raleigh, North Carolina, during high school, and the lonely people who would come in and request a table for one on Thanksgiving, dining alone in a booth on microwaved gravy and a slab of yellow-grey reconstituted turkey patty. "People want to be with other people on Thanksgiving," Cynthia says, trying to explain the pathological behavior of the Darryl's clientele. "And these people had no one to be with. I never understood why they didn't just push the tables together. All those

sad people in their individual booths—it was really depressing."
And Roby tells the saddest Thanksgiving story of all, about losing
a friend and her first Thanksgiving with friends gathered together
to mourn that loss. The stories people tell are universally sad,
notably so for a holiday that purports to be all about being grateful
for what you've got. Maybe that's appropriate in light of what it
commemorates historically, and maybe our attempts to recast it
as something else will never fully wash clean the fundamentally
tragic nature which has marked the occasion an occasion worth
marking. But Roby is a good egg, and her invitation is the only
thing standing between me and a table for one at some Darryl's on
the edge of town. Roby, who I know through punk, which is not a
family and entails no obligations, which may or may not care how
you look as long as you are punk on the inside, which certainly
could care less whether the lineage thrives and survives, whether
or not you become all that you threatened you would never be.

MANITOBA

Friday, early afternoon, cross-Canada drive. A very straight road between Winnipeg and Regina, stretching out grey to the horizon. The color of the sky matches. To the left and right you see rolling, sparsely populated prairie. There is a mild drizzle—Pete W. is driving in silence. "I like to wait until I need the stimulation to listen to music or something," he says. The road is so straight. I tell him to put the van in cruise control, let go of the wheel, and take a nap.

His theory about the music turns out to be right later on: delayed gratification is the way to go. Not a lesson I have yet been able to learn, eater of candy bars against my own best intention, a person who will put anything in his mouth that is presented to him, without hesitation. I have wised up to the correlations—the wrong food equals stomach ache, beer makes me depressed the next day—but not yet enough to modify the behavior, not enough to change the trajectory, which is ingrained.

Weird, insect-like threshing machines shamble their way across a furrowed field. Semis trundle by. Livestock of various sort dot the landscape. Lazy bovines, mostly; the occasional family of fiberglass deer, propped decoratively in front of small houses, double-wide trailers, little homes. From the vantage point of the insular interior of the band van, it makes you feel useless and anti-human, vaguely makes you wish for some act of catastrophic obliteration to make it all cease and desist. I suppose that's a regular, everyday human fantasy. Everyone longs for disruption from the everyday. But when you become active in that pursuit, when you undermine schedule and routine entirely, it makes you lonely in relation to the world around you. Regina: 362 KM

Stop for gas in Austin, Manitoba. Full service, one pump, a beautiful teenage girl doing the filling up. The town of Austin seems to be a half dozen shacks, several broken down rusting trucks and this gas station, which may serve as the hub of it all. The nerve center of the town, the gas station being itself also a service station, tire depot, and café. There are a few older guys straggling about the lot and a kid, maybe fourteen years old, pulls up on a motorized four-wheeler to get gas. I stand around and hope that maybe I'll have the opportunity to engage someone in conversation and so glean some further window into what life in Austin, Manitoba, might be like. No such luck. Gas comes to $100. Canadian.

The sun comes out. The landscape becomes more hilly, lush and green. I am wowed by it, goggle-eyed, staring out the long side window into a field of stunning, technicolor green. Next to me, Jessica stares at her laptop screen, focused and oblivious. She misses everything by her focus on phone and computer. Or, equally arguably, I miss everything by my inability to deal with either device. Between the two of us, we are missing the totality of human experience.

Another stop, this time at Ice Cream Island, middle of nowhere, Manitoba. Two confused teen boys vend ice cream with extreme inefficiency. There seem to be only teens and old people in these rural parts. I suppose that makes a certain amount of sense. The teens probably move away as soon as they can, or if they don't they probably get old pretty fast. Loitering, surly-looking young guys huddle in the office of the adjoining gas station, the presence of these tense balls of testosterone preventing me from my ritual shoplifting of maps as they are clustered around the display rack (tantalizing: Manitoba, Saskatchewan, Winnipeg). The provinces are big, open expanses of nothing, more topographical than urban/ highway. Perfect spaces, blank maps, almost.

As we approach Saskatchewan a sudden rainstorm erupts. The water thunders down upon us, wrathfully, as if in some unprovoked tantrum, as an act of punishment. Proving that it is not just what you eat and drink, what happens inside. The world is temperamental, too, the atmosphere, the air itself is askew with flux and emotion. Then we're through it, and the sun is out again. We're driving alongside a train, back through the countryside. The pavement dries and it's like it never happened.

LAS VEGAS

Morning in Las Vegas—New Mexico, that is. A bogus Vegas. An insane person stands out on the tarmac and watches me pump gas, cackling to himself maniacally. "What was your first name again?" he asks.

"Al," I say.

"Al Capone!" He breaks into hysterics, extends a hand and clutches mine. "Wow! You've got a firm handshake," he says. "You seem—you seem about ready to KILL somebody—!" He pulls a knife from his jacket pocket.

"Go ahead!" He yells. "Here! Here's a weapon!" He waves the knife at me, handle forward.

"No, no, I don't want to kill anybody," I say.

"Yeah, I know," he cackles quietly. "I'm just kidding." It's around six or seven in the morning; we stand outside and he explains himself. It doesn't make any sense. His story involves FBI agents, militia people, a deal gone bad, a carnival in Tucson he was supposed to work for which turned out to be a militia front, eyewitnesses, interrogations, the loss of his ID somewhere along the line.

The gas is pumped. "Good luck out there," I say.

"Hey, I got people like you," he says. "I got people like you, all around me. I'll be fine!"

BLACK SABBATH GREYHOUND CHRISTMAS

On the Hound headed home, December 24th, traveling through the empires of eternal void, as Black Sabbath said—penetrated by neon, punctuated by stars. Leaving Chicago in the middle of the night to be subsumed by the entrails of the great U.S. highway system, an endless drive to nowhere. Pennsylvania is a long state, horrendously wide from side to side. You can't even think about your location relative to destination while in Pennsylvania—it's demoralizing. In truth, though, a day in a bus is not that much worse than a day in your room. You can get about the same amount of stuff done, and watch the horrible landscape roll by as a bonus.

I had been sitting in my room on Christmas Eve, not doing much. I was avoiding the holiday, as has been my annual tradition since the disaster of a few years ago when my father remarried, and my attempts to get in the festive spirit (I was hanging bananas from the ceremonial tree) got me into a nasty altercation with the new step-parent. But that was years ago, and on this night, sentimentality welled up in me as I imagined the family, happily at home in North Carolina. I decided to pay a surprise visit. Half an hour later, I found myself at the downtown Greyhound station; leaving on the spur of the moment, this was my only financially feasible option.

The trick, on a long bus ride, is not to think about time, not to think of yourself as in motion, destined for anywhere. "Leave the earth to Satan and his slaves," advises Black Sabbath. The nozzle controlling the air vent has been ripped off by a previous passenger so that it can't be shut off, and the vent now spews freezing air on me. I rummage around for something to stuff into it and find, under my seat, a pair of leopard print socks left by a previous passenger. I stuff them into the vent.

I had been curious to see what sort of person takes an overnight Greyhound ride on Christmas Eve. Would there be exciting, sinister motivations for needing to leave town at such an odd time? But the answer, depressingly and obviously, is that it's mostly born again Christians. This became clear within a few minutes of departure from downtown Chicago, when the first person, an elderly gentleman in a crinkled suit, whipped out a bulky, well-thumbed and thoroughly hi-lighted jumbo print Bible and began shouting praises across the aisles. I looked around for someone to receive my exasperated eye roll but found no one. The entire bus was enraptured. Soon, Bible quotations and hallelujahs were flying back and forth between the aisles.

My instinctual reaction to loud displays of fervent proselytizing, of course, is to want to jump up and begin yelling counter-arguments in a louder voice. Fuck religion, as the song says, but in this case I immediately recognized that as an inhumane, culturally insensitive attitude, and also that I was hopelessly outnumbered. So, rather than yelling out Crass-style lyrics, I restrained myself and listened.

The Bible, even if taken as total fantasy, is no worse a fantasy text than J.R.R. Tolkien or Philip K. Dick. From a purely sales standpoint, it beats out all of these and even Stephen King's *The Stand*, another popular apocalypse-oriented text. There are some great action sequences: Moses parting the Red Sea, the destruction of Sodom and Gomorrah. Mel Gibson's fairly literal film version of the crucifixion of Christ was considered ultra-violent even by Quentin Tarantino standards, and then there's the Book of Revelations, still probably outside the ability of Hollywood special effects teams to approximate, featuring the population of earth under the leadership of Satan battling the army of heaven under the direction of Jesus while locusts and blood rain down. A close, literal reading of Revelations is the kind of thing that leads you to move to a cabin in Montana with thirty other people and start collecting guns and hoarding canned goods.

The birth of Christ, unfortunately, is no Book of Revelations. To put it mildly, it is not the most action-packed part of the Bible's story line. In fact, the New Testament is one of the few books written in any civilization to have childbirth as such an integral plot element and not include a sex scene. Rather, the conception of Christ takes place with an angel appearing and announcing sternly over the PA that Mary is now inseminated with the savior of mankind. She shrugs her shoulders and accepts it. That seems like an unhealthy relationship to authority.

In Pittsburgh, around two in the morning, there is a layover. The station is swarming with children; one exhausted mother leads her flock to the snack bar. "What do you want? Chips, crackers, cookies? What?" she says on autopilot. A very young girl stands pigeon-toed nearby, holding a newborn infant, eyes wide in numbed terror, both of them seeming far too fragile to be here.

Outside, I watch a couple get forcibly ejected from a bar across from the station. He is stumbling drunk, while she is belligerent. "Well, you don't smell it on me, and I've drunk as much as him! So why are you throwing me out?" she argues. The security guard is confused by her incoherent argumentation style, then tells her that you are not allowed to drink while in transit. "WHAT ELSE IS THERE TO DO?" she demands. I guess they've had a long layover. It seems to be only getting longer; they are told at the station that they'll have to wait until they've sobered up to board a bus. The man begins weeping at this news. She is inconsolable, and, when he tries to hug her, pushes him away and storms off angrily. He trails behind her sheepishly, shamed as she screams across the terminal, "You took me AWAY FROM MY HOME! FOR THIS!"

I find my seat again by locating the leopard print socks, flapping slightly in the air conditioner breeze. A girl with an astounding excess of glitter eye shadow boards, seats herself across the aisle, and begins making conversation with a guy wearing a puffy white coat and a backwards baseball cap, a few seats in front of me. The demographics are back to normal for this leg of the trip, and that's comforting. The bus resumes motion, and she switches seats to sit next to him.

A few hours later, just outside of Knoxville, Tennessee, the driver makes a grim announcement: passengers heading towards Raleigh-Durham might as well just give up hope. This line stops in Asheville, and there is no way we are going to make the connection. The news is delivered with bland authoritative fatality and is met by a general dull groan of resigned consensus. But there's even more bad news: the Greyhound station in Asheville is closed for the holiday, and it appears that when we arrive we will be stranded there. Another murmur of resignation ripples through the cabin. I look around in disbelief. What's it gonna take, I wonder, to get these people angry? They could be announcing a reroute through Anchorage, Alaska, and the Greyhound clientele would accept it as if it were one of the inescapable hassles of life. The riders have been pummeled into acceptance by years of this kind of merciless service. The revolutionary potential of the U.S. public is zero—still, to be stranding a busload of passengers on the Tennessee/North Carolina border on Christmas day seems particularly cruel and unusual, not to mention a bad idea from a public relations angle.

In any case, now that the cancellation of service to Raleigh-Durham has been announced, the jumbo print Bibles have been whipped out with renewed determination, and loud, animated invocations to the overbeing are gushing forth, asking that he intervene on behalf of this scheduling error of the Greyhound corporation. It's a lot to take at six in the morning after a mostly sleepless night and with the prospect of hitchhiking the rest of the day looming on the agenda of probable days' activities. Why, I wonder, aren't these Christians angered that the Greyhound bus company is fucking up their most sacred holy day? Despite the impressively oversized books, these are clearly casual readers. They haven't gotten to the end, to the big battle between good and evil. Here, among the average American non-extremist Christian, I can't help but think, *what a bunch of wimps!* These are not liberation theologists or ultra-right survivalists, nor do they bear much resemblance to the Apocalypse cult currently guiding U.S. foreign policy. These people have not embraced the deeper lesson of the Bible, which you get if you read it all the way through. It's not about waiting for Jesus to reroute the bus lines for you—it's about getting involved, picking a team, and getting ready to fight!

But my theology is disproven, because Jesus does in fact reroute the bus lines, or slows down time, or something. We make it to Asheville just in time to catch our connection. A miracle! People let loose copious hallelujahs and praises to the almighty as we hurry aboard the new bus, take our seats, and wait to depart. I hide behind the headphones, listening to Black Sabbath—*"through the universe the engines whine / could it be the end of man and time"*—rocking back and forth in my seat until a concerned Christian taps me on the shoulder to ask if I'm OK.

A few seats up, the girl with the glitter eye shadow has disappeared along with her puffy-jacketed partner. Their bags have been deposited in their seats, but they are gone, somewhere outside the bus. I let myself imagine that maybe they've given in, succumbed to all this talk of immaculate conception and to the magic of the moment, left their baggage behind and checked into a motel nearby. It would be nice to think of them, caution thrown to the wind, letting the luggage continue the sullen route without them. I cross my fingers that they won't show and that the rest of my trip there will be two glaringly empty seats in front of me, on this otherwise crowded bus, the abandoned bags a testament to spontaneous emotion and the possibility of sudden, life-altering circumstances which reroute you, against whose gravity you are powerless. I sit on the bus, waiting for it to lurch into motion, for my course to resume and theirs to veer off wildly into the unknown. And then, to my surprise, the doors do close, the bus actually does take off, and—before I can say anything—we're gone.

OPIATE OF THE MASSES
VS. MASSES OF OPIATES

Tucson, Arizona: "The Lord knows I'm sinnin', and sinnin' ain't right," sings a contemporary country crooner on the radio. "But me and the good Lord are gonna have a talk later tonight." A knee-jerk jab of the search button away, the mainstream alternative station offers the latest less-than-totally empathetic rock anthem by Weezer: "You've got your problems / I've got my hash pipe." And that pretty much summarizes the religious versus secular approaches to coping with life, problem solving through prayer versus problem solving through paraphernalia.

I've lost my keys and wallet. Having exhausted the two or three places I might possibly imagine they could be, I'm left with little recourse but to pray to some form of higher being for their return. I do this sometimes. Despite whatever set of beliefs and value systems I claim, I notice that I'm only an atheist when I'm being rational; as soon as I get panicked, I consult oracles and accept whatever theology will get me results.

In late spring 2000, I left my backpack, containing all my earthly belongings of any value, on a picnic table at a rest stop in southern Germany. I noticed the bag was missing two hours later. There seemed no chance of the backpack still being at the rest stop, but we drove the two hours back anyway, on the off chance that it might still be around. With nothing to do but obsess about my belongings during hours of tedious backtracking, I got desperate—I decided to accept religion into my life. My personal version of prayer is less hail Mary-oriented and more like haggling with some used-car salesman over the price of a dented Volvo station wagon, with my opening invocation to the Lord usually something along the lines of "Alright dude, it's me. Let's work out some kind of deal here." As I recall, the bargain brokered in this instance was that, in exchange for safe return of the backpack, plane ticket, passport, and traveler's checks, I'd cease all sinning in the traditional, old fashioned sense: I'd quit drinking alcohol and smoking marijuana and having physical relations with people whom I had little or no intention of marrying. Come on, big dude, I prayed, just hook me up, and I'm a believer.

It seemed like a fair deal, and apparently the Lord accepted my terms, because when I finally arrived at the rest stop, there was my bag, untouched and all items intact. It was a sign from heaven, and I knew what I had to do now to repay my debt.

"It's a miracle your bag is still here," said one of my traveling companions.

"Miracle?" I scoffed. "Man, I just got lucky this time."

That's the beauty of moral relativism. Backpack and all contents safely retrieved, I was an atheist again within minutes and reneging on my end of the deal within hours. The moment of crisis had passed and with it the need for help from a higher power. Now that I had my stuff back I could accept the world as chaos and randomness again, shouting drunken toasts to Charles Darwin on the dance floor as I went back into existential party mode.

So now, in Tucson, it seems clear that if there is a God, he's probably mad about the whole backpack situation, my failing to live up to my end of the deal and all, and he's decided to punish me by hiding my keys. An unfortunate turn of events in my spiritual life! Again, panic leads to the involuntary reaction, and I find myself hitting speed-dial on the hotline to Valhalla, muttering under my breath, "Alright, dawg. It's me again. You there? Listen, we gotta talk about this whole wallet thing." My prayers ring hollow this time, though—I've already lost spiritual cred with the backpack fiasco, and I can't imagine I'm going to be able to work out similar terms for this whole wallet/key deal. You can only pull the old "give me back my stuff and I'll believe in you" routine on the Almighty once; he doesn't fall for it the second time. No, I fear that my negotiation leverage is pretty low at this point. If I were God and I wanted lil' Bur to cease imbibing and cavorting, I'd certainly teach him a lesson in the form of a lost wallet and keys. Just as backpack retrieval equaled yes on the existence of New Testament yoga-instructor nice God, it seems clear that the deal in this case is that no keys and wallet = Old Testament vengeful God.

During moments of panic about the whereabouts of one's possessions, it becomes impossible to believe that there is not a higher schema in place governing your Job-like sufferings; it doesn't seem possible that your misfortunes could be a result solely of your own ineptitudes. No, there must be higher, persecuting forces at work. I have angered Jehovah, and he has confiscated my sub club cards and my van keys. I do not hold out hope of seeing these items again. Why me, Lord, why me? Aren't there more deserving fornicators and debauchers in this world who ought to be misplacing their car keys right at this moment? Why have I been singled out for the plague of locusts?

"Hey, is this your stuff?" says Tim, producing my keys and wallet from a bag where, the night before, I had stashed them and promptly forgotten all about it. "I was looking for duct tape and found this in here."

Hmmmm. Key and wallet retrieval. What does that mean? These signs from heaven are too hard to decipher. The early American puritans believed that you had to get a special invitational signal from heaven in order to gain entry into the afterlife, something like a rabid squirrel on your front lawn or a neat configuration of birds flying overhead. But modernity is an infinitely complex web of potential symbols and signs when you start looking for them, all conflicting and contradictory. Duct tape? The puritans never had to factor in such things to their theological paradigms. I can find no way to order the signs and signals, to make any sense of it all or derive a personal direction. I can't even flip coins; they fly out of my hand, invariably, and into the nearest storm drain.

•   •   •

Later that day, I'm transfixed by the tube in Tucson, watching CNN coverage of Mexican border drug busts (I believe it's CNN, although for all I know it may be some new reality "all drug busts all the time" cable channel). The War on Drugs is back in the headlines, suddenly, the 80's unfolding once again, except with "terror" as the -ism replacing communes as the evil being funded by drugs. The sudden resurgence of drug war propaganda, an 80's retro comeback the likes of which Mariah Carey could only dream of, disturbs me on a number of levels. On an abstract level, it just seems so impossibly tedious that history would so blatantly repeat itself—once as tragedy, once as farce, in Karl Marx's famous formulation, but in this as in so many things, Marx couldn't predict the advent of television reruns, and the population's subsequent willingness to accept repeats dozens of times. In any case, it's bad news on a global political level, but also bad news for me on a more concrete and personal level, as everyone else in the room is ignoring CNN and huddling around a Rand-McNally road atlas, planning out the logistics of a pharmaceuticals-smuggling road trip down to Mexico.

Before leaving town on the drug run, I consult my friend Bill Tsitsos on spirituality issues. Tsitsos can relate to my panicked lapses in atheism and admits, "I've just had to concede, lately, that I do believe in God, because I was having so many of those lapses that calling myself an atheist would make me a hypocrite. That's the irony of post-Enlightenment thinking," philosophizes Bill. "We have the scientific-rational power to overcome our reliance on God, but not to fill the void left by removing our reliance on God."

I would not consider myself an expert on the Enlightenment, but I believe that as a world-historical development it generally gets favorable reviews. Bill Tsitsos, however, is—as usual—on the contemporary cultural cutting edge with his retro revivalism: the rejection of enlightenment thinking in favor of tribal and religious warfare is totally 80's, though the mutually agreed upon Al Qaeda/Reagan-Bush political program suggests a return to the 880's more than the 1980's. Despite rhetorical shifts to downplay it, George W. Bush's proclaimed "crusade" has the same dogmatic fundamental undertones as every great religious extermination in history.

Religion makes no sense; it's illogical and speaks only to panicked, unenlightened people who can't find their keys. Politically, the atheist stance seems the only defensible one, and the only one which seems like it contains any hope of human survival, of transcending mutually assured genocide. We have to take responsibility for ourselves. But how do I reconcile this with the fact that God hooked me up with my backpack in Bavaria? And, further complicating matters, if I accept Tsitsos' "I pray therefore I believe" argument and choose to process as fact the idea that God revealed to me his desire that I cease my self-indulgent ways via an act of miraculous luggage retrieval, how then should I imagine the higher powers are taking my espoused political-atheist party-all-the-time program? Having received the signs from above, is it strategically advisable to align myself with the other team?

Wandering the seedy streets of Nogales, Mexico, a few hours later, I think about the TV footage of spy helicopters X-raying pickup trucks or the man caught with the pound of cocaine sewn into the skin of his leg. I do not understand the exact mechanics of the North American Free Trade Agreement, but, personally, I'd rather accept Mexico's cocaine than their environmental standards. And it seems like if we are going to impinge on unfettered commerce in this fashion and even devote television channels to the fettering, the Mexican government should demand that the CEOs responsible for shipping toxic waste to Mexico should have to smuggle it over themselves, sewn in flaps gouged out of their inner thighs.

The streets of Nogales are crowded with pharmacies, advertising 50% off antidepressants and prescription-free Viagra. We enter one such establishment, looking to purchase a piñata filled with valium, opioids, and other tour necessities. When we walk in the door, the pharmacist smiles brightly. "Hello!" he says. "Hippies?"

"No," we mutter.

He guesses again. "Punks?"

"Punks," Tim affirms.

Punks: with piñatas full of pills, the party program of the post-enlightenment dark ages, where the dollar is the state religion and pharmaceuticals are the manifestation of miracle, the synthetic spiritual solvent which fills the void left by a world based on rationality and calculation. This is the void which Bill feels and has to concede God in the face of; the void which drove George W. to his first career as alcoholic drifter before becoming born again as a fundamentalist Christian. Even our religious wars recognize the implicit parallel and quickly become drug wars, with anti-drug rhetoric adopting all the implicit race and class hostilities religious rhetoric is traditionally in charge of pushing. The empty future versus the bloody past, the scientists who say God is a combination of pills versus the zealots who say God demands that we kill. For the western world, medieval minds like George Bush will eventually prove atavistic. Religion is an irrational force, a flux in the mechanics of the market, which is too inefficient to be abided. As long as fundamentalists want to blow up abortion clinics or crash planes into trade centers, the dissemination of colas and plastic trinkets is impeded. But will humanity ever really accept plastic trinkets in the place of spirituality? Who can pick a side in the Jihad vs. McWorld war? And how long before the war on foreign ideology and belief trickles down to us here on ground level, how long before the war on terror equals the war on drugs and that equals renewed police intervention, once again, in the lives of ordinary U.S. citizens?

Answer: About three hours. Piñatas full of pills safely stowed in the backseat, we are cruising through Texas when the cops stop us at a random drug checkpoint. Prayer, again, crosses my mind as an option. But what deity to address? Whose team is God actually on? Ours? Theirs? Mine? Not mine, that's for sure. The missing wallet, I realize, was just an appetizer for the real wrath to come. The wages of sin is death. At the very least long-term incarceration. Drug-detecting dogs are barking and scratching at the doors of the van as the officer explains that he's onto us and that we should just hand over the drugs, and everything will be cool. "But if we have to search your van, you're all going to be in a lot of trouble," he explains. Oh, you don't know the half of it, officer. A sacrificial offering is required to the higher powers: I produce my remaining miniscule stash of crinkly Chicago marijuana and hand it over. "That's it?" the cop says, disappointed, holding the pitiful scrap of weed in his hand. He waves us off, aggravated, and we leave post-haste, the cop watching us in the rearview, shaking his head. Clearly he had been expecting a bigger bust, having mistaken us, I can only imagine, for hippies.

On March 16, 2004, I awake early, put on pants, drink some coffee, and prepare to perform my civic duty as an American national, and I'm not talking about submitting an application to join the cast of "The Real World" (that civic duty already checked off the list, mid-March 1999). Today is the Illinois primary election. Out of a household of four politically aware, left-leaning white males, I am the only one who will bother to vote in it. My subversive, political fanzine publishing roommate is not even aware that the primary is happening, but wastes no time making fun of me for bothering when I tell him why I'm up so early. "Kerry's going to get the nomination," he sulks, "Who cares? I'll vote for the lesser evil when the day comes, but I'm not leaving the house today."

This is a typical fallacy of the impatient Left, to be wrapped up in the aerial view, the three-ring circus presidential spectacle, and thus feel like anything but the most begrudging electoral participation is tantamount to calling a 900 number and casting your vote for which guest should be force-fed a sock on

Montel Williams. But democracy is not about the big picture, it's about the small shifts in power, down here on the ground level. "What's important is to vote for judges," I explain. "Chances are I will never be face-to-face with the President or, for that matter, a Senator or even a congressman. But a judge? Look at my face, man. I've got mothering instinct written all over me. When I get hauled into court, I want a woman judge!" As per my usual routine, I am planning to practice the "if they give you lined paper, write the other way" theory of voting. Rather than informing myself about the issues and meticulously studying the candidates' platforms, I prefer to vote from the heart, according to my most utopian dreams, not mundane fears about gradations in shade of evil. When I lived in Oregon, I had the pleasure of voting a straight Socialist ticket during the 1992 elections and even got to vote for my old friend Chris Phelps as a U.S. senate candidate (last time I saw Phelps was at a young communist meeting in Detroit—he was drunk and screaming, "can you imagine what the Middle Ages must have SMELLED like?"). At other times, I've enjoyed voting only for women. It might seem too biologically determinist to assert that if the gender ratio were reversed and all branches of government staffed 98% by women, the women would do a better job of running things—but who knows? How are we going to find out if we don't try it?

This election, I'm particularly excited about Republican Senatorial candidate Chirinjeev Kathuria, a Sikh Muslim whose main congruence with the sitting President's political platform is his obsession with "making space travel more accessible to the average citizen." Despite zip political experience, Kathuria proclaims himself "the most qualified person (for) the U.S. Senate," though he himself admits to his main political liability: "turban and beard." In fact, despite U.S. citizenship, a business degree from Stanford, and affiliation with the Republican Party, his website is still daily bombarded with geniuses hyperventilating about "Osama Bin Laden running for Senate in Illinois." Prominent Illinois Republicans have also expressed incredulity at a turban-wearing Sikh leading the party, and, while it is doubtful that these politicians will one day be seen, from the vantage point of the multi-ethnic, religiously harmonious Mars colonies of 2520, as the twenty-first centuries' equivalent of southern anti-abolitionists, who knows for sure?

Things change in small and incremental ways. Up North Avenue, towards Western, and my old apartment, under which address I'm still registered to vote. I haven't gotten too far in the three and a half years I've lived in Chicago—I'm still a bike ride from every place I've ever lived, and I still have the same tenuous job I got my first week in town. Myopic Books has moved up the street a few blocks; a shoe store has closed and a Starbucks coffee has opened on the corner. Tony Lazzara tells me that this corner, North and Damen, used to be really scary, even ten years ago. "When I was a kid, this was the only corner where my dad would hold me by the back of the neck," he says. "It was like he was scared that someone was just going to run up and grab me right in front of him."

Ironically, it is precisely this corner, in fact mere blocks away from my current residence, where I would have been living, had my application to "The Real World" gone through. Wicker Park, now better known as the set for *High Fidelity* than as a particularly dangerous intersection in the vehicular homicide capital of the U.S., had gentrified by 2000 into enough of a bohemian playground to warrant reality programming. I never watched an episode of "The Real World: Chicago," but I did end up participating in the show in a weird vicarious way: like many residents of the Wicker Park area, I engaged in public protests outside the building, threw rotten fruit at the wall, was gleeful to see paintball splatter on the door, or citizens' jeering and harassing the cast in the streets. That none of this apparently ever aired on the program is a testament to the "reality" being peddled—but in any case, as a first impression of Chicago, it was inspiring. *You can gentrify this street,* the populace seemed to be saying, *but we still live nearby and it's not a long walk over here to mug you.*

Western Avenue, the straightest street in America (from a road atlas point of view), is considerably more run-down than North and Damen, but here, too, change is perceptible: the food mart underneath my old apartment has closed down, replaced by a left wing bookstore. This corner is where I first learned to accept the sound of gun shots as part of regular urban life; the left wing bookstore, thus, registers as the antithesis of the Real World building. Here amongst the off-camera wreckage of reality are the proponents of the Fantasy World, peddlers of the highest hopes, the most uncompromising stances. Across the street is the fire station where, today, the gears of democracy are slated to churn. The left wing shopkeep stands outside his store and smiles at me as I lock my bike up. "Voting today?" he nods encouragingly. He seems a little giddy, like a Catholic on Easter, half-aware that he is watching a ritual, a simulacrum of the real, and half-aware that this is the core of his belief-system, the moment when we divide between the saved and the damned.

The fire station is depressingly empty. Volunteers, mostly elderly ladies, sit at a folding table stocked with donuts. "Donut?" a volunteer says, and then, her priorities clearly sorted, asks me for my name and voter registration card.

"Democrat or Republican?" she asks.

"Do you have any other options?" I ask.

"Non Protestant," she says. That description is closer than the other two, but it still confuses me. "Non Protestant?" I repeat, uncertainly.

"Non Partisan," she clarifies, reading the form a little more closely. "Sorry."

"Either way, I'll take it," I say.

In the voting booth, I begin at the bottom of the ballot, working my way up from the more meaningful choices of water reclamation district commissioners and judicial subcircuits to the fantastic world of congressional, senatorial, and presidential races. I am torn as to whether I should vote according to the Illinois Progressive Voters' Guide included with the *Chicago Reader* or whether I should just go for it and vote for the people with the craziest names. Fortunately, perusal of the voter guide reveals an exact 1:1 correlation between the two, and thus Xochitl "So-She" Flores becomes my choice for water commissioner, while Barb Burchjolla and Bonnie Berger-Neel become my delegates to the democratic national nominating convention, narrowly beating out Daniel Birkhahn-Rommelfanger.

Finally, at the top of the ballot, I come to the crux of my roommate's argument, the choices (or rather, lack of reasonable ones thereof) for President of the U.S., all lesser and all relatively evil. And here I am stumped. Illinois is a Midwestern state, and, while not quite as boring as Iowa, it is still generally considered culturally wonder bread enough that the citizens are allowed a few wing-nut choices, just to prove we have those choices, before we do the sensible thing, eliminate all the interesting people, and send the electoral process south. The flailing Howard Dean is still on this ballot, as are Kucinich and Clark—but who cares? Isn't a vote for any of these people, regardless of their views, a Ralph Nader vote, a statistical throwaway? Realistically, the funniest name on the presidential ballot is probably a tie between Al Sharpton and Lyndon LaRouch. The only 98 percenter is Carol Moseley Brown, but her name isn't really funny at all. Can I vote for a Carol Brown when mine eyes have seen the glory of a Xochitl Flores?

My roommate is right, I suppose; in November I'll vote pragmatically, for Anyone But Bush, as the not-too inspirational slogan says. The idea that my last presidential vote, for Nader, was irresponsible, that a 2% showing in the polls equals an outrageous display of unconscionable idealism on the part of people like me, is something that both the Democrats and Republicans would love me to believe. And, OK, I'll accept that our backs are against the wall. The first four years of Bush Jr. make one long for the diplomacy and level-headedness of Reagan, and it is not clear that the world has room to inch another four years' closer to Armageddon. In November, it will be serious, if for no other reason than that democracy itself was compromised in the shady electoral riggings of 2000, and that another victory for Bush may signal the real defeat of the principles, utopian as they may be, upon which the U.S. is premised. But these are the primaries. This is where we put our best foot forward, where we vote with our hearts, not the dark fears of the rational, pragmatic mind. And there's always the write-in option. If it's a white bread, presidential-sounding name you people want, I'm willing to compromise. In ball-point, I letter the name in neatly: A-N-D-R-E B-E-N-J-A-M-I-N, aka ANDRE 3000. Depositing the ballot in the box, I take a deep breath and realize that I have never cast a more earnest vote in my life.

MC DONALDS FINDS
MISSING INGREDIENT

The front page of the *Chicago Tribune* today features the headline "McDonalds finds missing ingredient" alongside a photo of grinning CEO Charlie Bell posing with an equally elated-looking low level employee. Assuming this missing ingredient to be metaphorical, I read the story, wondering what combination of factors is going to be touted as responsible for what the *Tribune* calls "one of the most stunning turnarounds in corporate history"—new all-robot kitchen staff? Aggressive marketing to the infirm and elderly? Mad-cow neutralizing agents which have allowed the company to buy cut-rate infected beef?— but no, it turns out it's an actual literal ingredient that has been found. In fact, a whole recipe: the "special sauce," corporate urban legend of the most profound and mythic, otherwise known as some combination of mayonnaise, ketchup, and flavor-enhancing "secret ingredients." The exact chemical makeup of the "special sauce" is a closely guarded industrial secret, so much so that even high level executives of the company are unaware of its exact composition. But retired CEO Fred Turner "could taste it," apparently, when "corporate headquarters changed the recipe to cut costs." Gastronomically enraged, Turner confronted the board of directors, who confessed that the recipe for the secret sauce had actually been lost completely, misfiled somewhere within the bureaucratic ring of the scientific sub-community employed by the corporation. Without the bewitching, hypnotic taste of the flagship sauce at its disposal, the company's mind-control grip on the populace had begun to weaken, stocks had plummeted, and only the elderly and nostalgic still pined for the days when the cheeseburgers cost ten cents and the sauce had that extra "tang."

McDonald's miraculous economic recovery is the feel-good story of the twenty-first century: "losing the special sauce meant a loss of connection with the company's very roots," the *Tribune* tells us. And thus, an internal accounting of error has been undertaken, wrongs have been righted, ratios restored and roots reconnected. The special sauce is back. In an unrelated article, meanwhile, the United Nations environmental committee (UNEP) announces at an emergency meeting that the world population of apes are being "eaten into extinction." Klaus Toper, UNEP executive director, puts it in terms the Iron Maiden fan can understand when he states that "the clock is standing at one minute to midnight" for a group of animals who "share more than 96 per cent of their DNA with humans."

Ninety-six, that's a high percentage, probably about as much as I would have guessed I share with the average human. I can't help but feel an affinity for my 96 percent relatives, the gorilla and the chimpanzee, numbers now dwindling low enough so as to be extinct between 2010-2020. I feel like a chimp most of the time: trainable to an extent (I can tie my own shoes) but not fully functional (I can't work your cell phone). But should I be eaten for this offense? Senegal and Ghana, for instance, are estimated to have 200-400 chimpanzees left, mostly in remote regions where, in the human populations' defense, it's hard to find a McDonalds and chimpanzee is a more viable fast food option. Human beings have annihilated the chimpanzee's natural habitat almost in its entirety and arguably have annihilated their own natural habitat in its entirety as well, although we've thoughtfully left food marts and vending machines with bottled water around for the apes up to the 97% genetic standard.

You can almost feel a certain level of sympathy for the aging McDonald's executives, old men who are confused about how to access their email accounts, who still operate on the ancient standards of what they can smell and taste. The "secret sauce" cover story in the *Tribune* is feel-good reporting, designed to inspire confidence in the somnambulant twitchings of the flaccid American economy, a hack job no doubt copied directly from the corporate press release, oozing with sentimentality and the simplistic notion that our present ills are a result of losing our way, of straying from the time-tested recipes and customer satisfaction formulas which made this country great in the first place. One wonders if a man like Fred Turner doesn't ever feel like a chimp himself, clinging to the shadow of a world that once was. Turner developed the staples of the McDonald's menu alongside founding hamburger mogul Ray Kroc, fine-tuned the condiments and side orders, and helped usher in a new voraciousness in multinational corporate expansion. The culinary history of the twentieth century, after all, is the history of fast food's ascension to global dominance. Nostalgia for the days when things tasted better is too little too late, like pining for an orangutan in 2025. Live by the food chain, die by the food chain: suddenly the heads of McDonalds find themselves the chimps, the atavistic apes in the way of progress, mumbling lamely about tradition and quality as the bulldozers of the bottom line roll in.

I'm glad I made the cut, I guess, to be one of the mammals who might find a sandwich improved by a secret sauce rather than being better tasting if served with a secret sauce. Still, the prospect of the uninhabitable world I'll be stuck with until I chimp out between 2030-2050 is not a pleasant one. Klaus Toepfer seems to feel some remorse, too: "We will be destroying a bridge to our own origins," he laments about the coming ape extinction, "and with it a part of our own humanity." Ah, yes, humanity. There is a darker side to this whole story, even: Jim Cantalupo, the chief executive who helped institute the turnaround at McDonalds once Fred Turner restored unto them the secret of the special sauce, keeled over dead of a heart attack on April 19, 2004, in the middle of the miracle recovery. Charlie Bell (CEO pictured on the *Tribune* cover) has taken the reigns, restoring calm and confidence for a good two weeks before being diagnosed with colon cancer. He is optimistic about chemotherapy: "The doctors have told me I won't lose my hair," he says. "This is a good thing, because I'm anxious to be the first McDonald's CEO in decades who actually has a full head of hair." Ketchup, initially introduced to the condiment world as a cover for rotten meat, then formally accepted into the vegetable kingdom by the late Ronald Reagan, now an indispensable ingredient of American cuisine, even a part of American "culture" or "heritage" when mixed with mayonnaise and eleven to thirteen secret ingredients: front page news on the cover of the *Tribune*. I'll miss the apes.

ROAD RAGE

The State of Illinois has suspended my driver's license. One more indignity, yet another assertion of my inability to function as a normal adult human, but, on the other hand, one less responsibility, one less logistic to worry about. Losing my driver's license, when coupled with my recent chiropractic problems, has transformed me into the kind of guy who will only play the show if you drive me there, set up the amps for me, and gingerly place the guitar around my neck right before it's time to begin. I have always wanted to be that type of person. If fame could not provide such a state of affairs, at least now incompetence and physical dilapidation has.

As to how this sad state of affairs came to be, one must track down my column of mid 2004, where (you might recall) my housemates were in the midst of berating me for participating in the sham democracy of voting in the primary elections. Democracy, in the broad national sense, having been retired from the playing field during the 2000 elections (if not long before), the theory being popularly expounded at that time was that participation in the charade was tantamount to endorsing the de facto coup d'état of the Cheney-Halliburton regime and that the intake of oxygen which would transpire while traipsing over to the voting booths was a waste of lung capacity better saved for bong hits around the apartment. Perhaps a valid point, although for me the issue was less ideological and more pragmatic. "Look at my face!" I had argued, "I've got mothering instinct written all over me! *When I go to court, I want a woman judge!*"

And indeed, when I was hauled into traffic court, finally, for a minor traffic offense (running a stop sign) I got lucky: I got a woman judge. Who knows? Maybe I even voted her in. In any case, my theory turns out be wrong: having a representative of the fairer sex presiding over me did not help me out one bit.

What went wrong? Well, OK: my behavior in the courtroom was, admittedly, a little erratic. Neither the judge nor the public defender seemed particularly out to get me; both seemed to have only my best interests at heart and seemed to want to guide me towards the path of least resistance—a guilty plea, acceptance of a small fine, and back out the door. This was clearly the moment to bow my head, nod meekly, accept a slap on the wrist, and depart. Somehow, though, once on the stand and under oath, I just couldn't help it, something came over me, and I vehemently professed my innocence, began lying my ass off, making up crazy excuses, rambling incoherently. I felt, as I did this, almost literally possessed, taken over by some evil imp who moved my mouth and limbs for his own devious purposes. To what end? Somehow, in that moment, I was overcome by the conviction that I had done nothing wrong, that I was exempt from the laws of the land, from a social contract I had never agreed to sign, and... and... As I snapped out of the spell in the middle of the phrase "exempt from the laws of the land," up there on the podium, under oath and on tape, with the judge, the public defender, and the arresting officer all staring at me with confused incredulity, a realization crept in: I had fucked up. Blown it. And the feeling this elicited in me, rather than horror or shame, was just dull recognition.

"Uhh... anything else to add?" her Honor solicited cautiously. I shrugged my shoulders. The evil imp had all kinds of things left to say, but I was awake now. I was back in control.

I wish I could describe this courtroom fiasco as an isolated incident, but in fact the evidence against my mental health stability seems to be mounting. Looking back through my writing over these past few years I notice a pattern emerging: continual reference to these moments of demonic possession, moments where I can not fully account for nor explain my behavior. In short, moments where I am not in control of my actions. A portrait emerges of a scrambled, dysfunctional person. The writing down of it, perhaps, is the act of reasserting control, of bringing the insanity in line with the rules of structure and grammar, syntax, descriptive language. When it works out, it is this dichotomy between form and content that makes an anecdote entertaining. But consider that it is me that this is actually happening to, that you are laughing at a person too maladjusted to do something as simple as hold down a driver's license, and that... or perhaps you shouldn't. Maybe this is too much information? TMI?

"Ah, the meta-column," fellow writer Jon Strange once advised me, back when I first got this gig, but still didn't know what to write about, and was throwing out ideas at him. "The column about why you write a column. Bad idea. Nothing worse, actually, except maybe re-typed tour diary." Sound advice, but by column #3 I was re-typing my tour diary and now, here, I find myself failing at goal #1. I'm getting meta, and, like lying to the judge, even as I do it, I can't seem to muster up shock or horror. No, I feel comfortable. I'm fucking up. Here we go again.

ROME LOPE

My mom tells me that Italy has dissolved its mental institutions and released all the lunatics, the result of a budget cut, just as Ronald Reagan did in the U.S. in the 1980's. It hasn't really changed the ambience all too much. You can't really tell a difference on the streets of Rome, where the number of free-range lunatics seems about consistent with any other time I've been here in my life. When I visited here about ten years ago, there was a guy who would walk from piazza to piazza, shrieking in blood-curdling and never-ending horror at some view he alone had into the abyss, his eyes bloodshot and bulging. People called him "the screamer;" no one seemed particularly put out by his appearances, which you could hear coming from miles away— or, if they were put out, they never suggested any course of action for dealing with him more proactive than hoping he'd go away soon.

The number of free-roaming insane in the capital city of the former great imperial power of Rome seems to have maintained a steady level since my twenties and since my early teens and, as far as I can imagine, since the time of Christ, when the loin-clothed followers of that particular doomsday cult leader were just one more sub-grouping of swarthy street lunatics, roaming the street in a pack looking for change, rattling it in a tin cup. It's hard to envision the landscape without the lunatics; they give it color and their jerky, incoherent movements give the whole scenario a wobbly, drunken orbit, as if they've knocked the planet slightly out of axis with their bad magnets, creating an off-center, lurching gravity which holds you tight to the earth for a moment, then sends you reeling, giddy and free, the next.

It's hard to be unhappy with the weather as nice as this, though I try and try. Standing at the Piazza Navona with Dave, watching people pass us by, I want to pull my hair out in fistfulls, roll my eyes back into my head, froth and point, crazy and thus totally invisible to the pedestrians navigating the square. I marvel at the people. What a world to produce such specimens! What a city to collect them all! I elbow Dave, narrating like it's a nature show. My overzealous tour guide mode is all an act, of course, to keep from my usual modus operandi when in the city of aqueductal emotions, weeping openly, which is what I no doubt would be doing if incognito and left to my own devices on the sinewy side streets, which switch names literally from block to block, so that trying to keep oriented in the maze becomes impossible. Every streetlet here is named after a different celebrated Italian person with Roman numerals after his name, an Allesandro VIIII or Guilliano XXVII, so that the maze becomes a maze of important human names, a labyrinth borne from the admirable notion that there are so many people who deserve to have a street named after them that, given the finite number of streets available in the city, to give anyone more than a tiny stretch of street seems unfair to the others. On these sinewy streets, I would have stumbled along like a blind man, arms outstretched, gnashing my teeth and pulling my hair, one more Minotaur in the maze. But I can't behave so crazily in front of Dave. What would he think?

It's OK. I have done the sad, drunken lope around Rome plenty of times, enough to know it by heart, and it's almost just motions now, ceremony. I can mouth the curses and oaths to myself, and point out the monuments while I'm at it. The Pantheon, dating back to the emperor Tiberius, once a temple of Pagan worship, the first such temple to use as a Christian church, now the site of the tombs of the early Italian kings, also the burial site of the painter Raphael, about whom my ex-girlfriend, on this very spot three years ago, said, "Oh, that's my favorite Ninja turtle." I don't tell Dave that part, though, that would be what they call Too Much Information. It would blow my cover, reveal the dark inner monologues, vying for air-time in the corner, crowded out by the bright and cheerful exterior monologue issuing forth.

Here, then, out of the nebula of the unknown ahead, emerges a blueprint for a future life that I could envision for myself: tour guide. It combines all my interests: walking around, lecturing people, being the center of attention. I could take people around, explain the objects to them, show them where to get the best ice cream afterwards. It's what I'd be doing anyway; it wouldn't seem like work. Yes, here is something I could see myself doing—if only it didn't involve reliance on the legs, which will surely fail me. My knees are weak, ready to give up the ghost long before my blabbering mouth will be. Some plan must be worked out for the future—there are too many slopes to slip down if one isn't careful, too many potential ignoble fates to befall the listless. At the Coliseum, you see old drunks dressed up in the uniforms of Roman Centurions, their costumes rented out and wine-stained, posing for photographs with tourists. I watch one Centurion for a while, so bored and drunk he forgets to put on his helmet when a timid Japanese family approaches him. The plumed helmet lays forgotten in the grass as he stumbles upright, realizes that he can't locate his sword either, and ends up posing with them anyway, making a peace sign and grinning sheepishly. In his metal mini-skirt and red cape, with a good week of stubble on his chin, he looks completely deranged. But this is one of the sane ones, doing what he has to do to survive.

STORAGE SPACES

I have embarked on a voyage into a dark sphere of existence, sunk to a new low. I have entered the world of storage units. "Occupant waives any claim for emotional or sentimental attachment to the stored property," reads my rental agreement at Lincoln Park Self Storage, where I am keeping my records, books, clothes, and everything I have ever written or drawn, amongst other items I am now contractually barred from having sentimental attachments to.

This brings up a philosophical quandary. When one identifies oneself as a "non-materialist," what else is there to hold on to but sentiment? Boxing up your belongings can be a jarring experience; all that emotional attachment, the abstract and unquantifiable meaning which gives things value, reduced to blankness, broken down to component categories—clothes, books, records, paper. It's like having a dead body suddenly on your hands. Just yesterday, it was breathing, living, telling jokes, or wallowing in childhood hang-ups. Now it is inanimate: bones, skin and hair, an object taking up space.

Wandering the halls of the storage facility, one is struck by the silence, the vacuum of lifelessness, interrupted only occasionally by the creaking wheels of a hand cart, shuffling someone's belongings in or out. Banks of video monitors in the office verify the lack of activity everywhere, like a high-tech mummy's tomb, filled with items for some later use, in the occupants' next incarnation. The clerk at the desk tells me about the weird things he's seen people store here: rooms full of worthless and water-damaged furniture, boxes full of children's toys, things which one only keeps because of the sentiment attached. He explains the clause in the contract: "It's just to protect us, in case, god forbid, someone runs amok with a flamethrower or something."

Up on the fourth floor, where my belongings are kept, there is a big bay window with a great view. Since moving my stuff here, I've had to come by on occasion to retrieve this or that item, and it is always nice, on a sunny day, to spend a few minutes staring out the window at the gleaming towers of downtown. Summer is ending, soon to lurch into a season of eternal darkness, but for now the sky exudes the feeling of endless potential. On these occasions, I try to retrace my path, to figure out how I ended up here, wandering the blank, unsentimental halls like some disembodied wraith.

In the apartment I'd been living in until just recently, the gas bill had gone unpaid, running free and registered under "occupant" for nearly two years. One day, as the first hint of chill hung in the air, the gas was finally shut off. It was the final nail in the coffin of an already crappy apartment, and rather than pay the outstanding billions of dollars on two winters with the heaters cranked and the windows open, the household decided to disband. I had enough touring plans lined up for the fall that any new place I moved into would be a de facto storage unit, and so I figured why not just go all the way with it?

Having moved out of the living space, the only type of space I now occupy, other than storage, is practice, and I sometimes in fact make the mistake of referring to my storage space as my practice space, having to catch the slip by calling it my "practicing to be a person" space. It does seem a little unfair: my own body is not worthy of housing, apparently, but these unwieldy amplifiers and enormous speaker cabinets, many of whom are themselves in far less functional form than I, have somehow finagled their way into an air-conditioned room.

Which brings me to my last category of material excess here on the physical plane: musical equipment. Though I am not even close to the upper echelons of excess when it comes to hoarding such gear, I do have my share, including a few objects which I can not possibly lift and transport on my own. I don't like that feeling; it's like owning a bunch of refrigerators, or a herd of elephants. This physical fact, the sheer weight of it all, ties me already from the get-go to others, who will need to help me get the objects up and down the stairs. And from there your dependency only grows, because actually turning the devices on and making noises come out of them in the company of others will bind you to them, enmesh and ensnare you in ways you could have never predicted, desired, or foreseen.

With music equipment, I tow my standard anti-material line, that as much genius is spewed from the speakers of cheap practice amps as there is uninspired, by-the-numbers aural wallpaper from professional backlines—it's the sentiment expressed, not the material means of expression, that's important. On the other hand, it's hard to deny that rock music is about 50% ability—what you are actually playing—and 50% tone. It's not hard to play the basic chords of an AC/DC song, but it will only sound like AC/DC through a Marshall amp. I can't deny that if I want to induce the slightly nauseating, chest-cavity rattling bass feeling which first gave me transcendental experiences when I stood in front of Corrosion of Conformity's speaker cabinet at the Brewery in North Carolina, circa 1985, I'm going to need an 8-10 speaker cabinet, literally about the size and weight of a small refrigerator. Nor can I deny sentimental attachments to the one I have, which was played that very same night in 1985 by the Ugly Americans, and which I purchased a few weeks later, date of birth stamped on the back of the speakers, the cabinet born a few months before I was, in the spring of 1971.

On tour, the music gear will be stored under a wooden-framed loft-bed, upon which I will not be able to sleep, because when I get up there I can not help but morbidly obsess on the idea of the van flipping, and all that weight, all those thousands of pounds of gear, crushing me flat against the ceiling. At the same time, how can I not feel attachment to it all? Born in 1971, like me, the cabinet is a slightly off-brand, a Traynor, and I can identify with that too, it seems like the amp equivalent of the slightly wrong hand-me down clothes I'd wear in junior high. The places we've been, the conversations we could have, the slightly nauseated feeling we've induced, all over the U.S.A.

Besides your own death, the other all-consuming fear of tour is having your gear stolen, an apocalyptic but unfortunately all-too common occurrence. Bands that have their equipment stolen, in my experience, either succumb to that physical reality and disband or persevere and become stronger for it. They recognize their essential bandness as something amorphous, a common bond, a need for expression which transcends the means of transmission. You have to admire people with that much conviction in the non-material. Still, it must be a bizarre feeling: all of a sudden, you are a bunch of people, with a collective set of muscle memory, that, when actualized, would produce songs, only you've lost the means to take that step into the physical world. Is a singer who loses their voice still a singer? Is a band without equipment a band?

•   •   •

Dave's brother Tom in North Carolina came home one night to find his house engulfed in flames. Books, papers, clothes, records, musical equipment—and a huge, painstakingly assembled collection of films, occasionally screened around town, now laying on the pyre. Stacks of 8 millimeter, super 8, and 16 millimeter reels, old educational films, clunky 50's propaganda, found arty weirdness, and his own projects; all of this evaporating before his eyes. The results of nothing so spectacular as a flame-thrower-wielding psychotic, Tom's house fire was the result of a halogen lamp tipping over. A simple, innocuous object, purchased for a few bucks at a thrift store, devoid of any value beyond its simple functionality, generating light and heat. It had destroyed everything. There was nothing to do now but begin again.

Tom had a video camera with him and, not knowing what else to do, filmed. When watching the footage of the building, his home, dematerializing in a howling blaze of heat and light, one gets a vicarious sense of both the horror and the elation the fire must have elicited. Such a sight is a primal fear realized and the deepest, most unspoken wish fulfillment, both at once. Everything. Gone. My dad described the feeling of losing his own parents as having a weird kind of lightness, a lifting of weight he hadn't known was there. Within the horrible aloneness of shedding the only constants you've known your whole life, there is something uplifting, a realization of self, of you being you, independent of anything outside of yourself. There is a freedom in being cut loose into the world, disconnected from bonds so familiar you would never have thought of them as binding until they ceased to be.

Were my storage space to be immolated, I would miss my clothes the least, certainly. The whole idea of sentimental attachment to clothing, though it applies to one or two T-shirts, does not on the whole make any sense to me. The books I might miss, though there are libraries in which I could find most of them, and I rarely reread books in any case, so that the shelf/cardboard box full of them is little more than sentiment, a bunch of spines within which you can book-end my identity, learn a little something about me as you peruse the shelf.

The boxes of papers have the lowest resale value and would be the quickest to burn, and I can scarcely conceptualize their loss. It's the closest I can imagine to my own eradication short of being caught in the burning building myself. Once, I misplaced a crate full of journals I'd been keeping for years. I searched for them for a few weeks, before conceding that they were gone, had probably been thrown out or something. I keep notes on things mainly because my memory is bad. When I would look back on these writings, I was often astounded by how warped my remembered version was compared to what I had written down at the time. I'd find that my version of events was completely wrong, or discover details which I'd completely erased, which would have ceased to exist for me had I not made some record of them. Now, with this surrogate memory gone, I had to fundamentally re-envision my life. One wonders why one even bothers living if so little attention is going to be paid while you're doing it. Keeping those journals was a way of holding onto some form of basic truth, of what I had done and what I had thought of it. Now that they had disappeared, wasn't I erased too? Is a life without documentation a life at all? But, in some very small way, I felt that weightlessness that my dad had described. Even divorced of memory, of my own past, I was still somehow me.

Now, the weight of holding on to what was behind me had been removed, and all that remained was the present and the unwritten future. Then the crate turned up, under a staircase or something, and there was that awkward relief relatives feel at a funeral when, in the middle of their grieving, the body sits up in the casket and proclaims itself to have only been napping.

And as for the records, well, these have been the subject of more than one late-night insomniac debate: if the house were to catch fire, which ones would I grab? Or would I just accept that the collection was lost, unsalvageable, and that the real question, here, was which one to put on and listen to last as the smoke and flames crept closer? (answer: probably Black Sabbath's "Black Sabbath," on account of the lyrics: "watch as those flames get higher and higher... oh no, please god help me!... Noooooo!")

• • •

Back in Chicago, early December. Walking the halls of the practice space on Superior and California. Listening to the cacophonous sound-montage of a million bands all playing at once, with black metal melding into ska melding into a cover version of Survivor's "Eye of the Tiger" as you walk down the hall, past the maddening schizophrenic din of dashed hopes and unachievable dreams, I am reminded of the silence in my storage space. Despite offering what would seem, on first listen, to be opposite sensory experiences, the basic gist of both buildings is the same. The noise, like the silence, makes the listener feel generic. Just as my boxes of papers are stripped of meaning by being placed in proximity with everyone else's boxes of molding personal items, it is difficult to keep your own personal motivations for making music in mind when you are confronted with the demographic overview. You catch glimpses of rooms covered floor to ceiling in splayed-crotch centerfolds, outside of which loiter guys stroking their pony-tails and eagerly discussing the terms of a recording contract or the load-in time at some local club. These people are your fellow musicians, you realize, dreaming the same dream as you.

While it can be fun to travel the country and sleep in a van or on a friends' couch, it is not nearly as good a time to come back home and sleep in a van or on a friends' couch. All that freedom starts to feel like martyrdom. I find myself hanging out at the practice space at odd hours, often very early in the morning, when it's still relatively quiet—and sometimes, around nine o'clock, somewhere down the hall, I'll hear an alarm clock go off. Someone is living in their practice space, waking up early to go to work or to just get out of there before the noise becomes unbearable. The sound of that alarm seems unfathomably depressing. What could be worth it, what could be going on in that person's life to weigh out that life decision, to make such a level of discomfort seem sensible and the best option? This person seems committed to the path of most resistance.

Tonight, for some reason, Tony Lazzara and I have decided to play a show at an art gallery—spontaneous, semi-improvisational, and "just for fun," as we keep insisting, implying with the phrase some other, more insidious motive one might have for such behavior. In truth, I haven't had one second of fun, from the pure terror of booking the show and having it confirmed without having any idea of what to perform, to enlisting Tony's as the drummer, to our hasty and nerve-wrackingly scant practices. Now, as we pack up our gear and prepare to carry it down four flights of stairs, things seem less party atmospheric than ever, and Tony reminds me optimistically that we have kept in the spirit of the thing, as we'd originally discussed it: we have kept it fun and are doing it just for the sake of the music. I don't remember having had this conversation with him but have to concede that it sounds like the kind of thing I'd probably say. Our mutual friend Cayce has volunteered to help carry the Traynor cabinet down the stairs. "I just came along because I like lifting things," he jokes. "I like the lifestyle."

Outside the space, we grit our teeth against one of the coldest nights of winter so far this year—and then can't help laughing again at the absurdity of this act, the futility of what we're involved in. When we get to the staircase we'll have to climb at the art gallery across town, we'll laugh even harder. Anything worth doing, the axiom seems to be, is about ten times more effort than the results will warrant. Your most sensible option, in terms of effort to happiness ratio, is probably to stay at home. Home? This is where the anti-material ideology breaks down, reveals itself to have been secretly renting a storage unit full of childhood doodads and oversized stuffed animals while standing on the street corner in a loincloth pretending to possess nothing. There is a difference, after all, between playing air guitar and playing guitar: the guitar.

And the amp. And the enormous speaker cabinet. And learning to play the guitar. And then carrying all that stuff somewhere. It's all so much more difficult than it should be. What sounded like spontaneous outbursts of sound and feeling on the records has revealed itself, over time, to be the product of astounding amounts of labor, blown speakers, money down the drain, lives wrecked, vans loaded and unloaded, back problems, knee injuries, etc. To what end? Once you get that speaker cabinet up the stairs, your reward will be that you might briefly get to forget about the stairs you'll have to go back down. Tonight I'll get it, the feeling of blast off, transcendence, a breaking of the bonds which tie me to the mundanity of the objects. The trick is to make it appear effortless, to create an illusion so powerful that it's ideological, that it conveys your irrational ordering of the world, a world without weight, enough so that you fool everyone and perhaps even fool yourself. And then it's back down the stairs.

PART
TWO

DO NOT SWALLOW CONTENTS

writing for

HEARTATTACK ZINE

While gyrating suggestively on the dance floor of "the Bootie Barn" in Tampa, Florida—*woah!* Perhaps I should back up a bit. That may be a little too jarring an opening sentence, especially in lieu of the fact that this may well find itself inserted between a vegan recipes column and an investigation of DIY hedge ornamentation, causing brains of readers to make a noise not unlike changing gears in a manual transmission car without using the clutch—OK, look: one has to understand, culture is all relative, and, while on a trip to, say, Washington DC, I might be somewhat titillated to be in the presence of bouffant-sporting scenesters at a punk rock show, that doesn't take away from my desire to see the Smithsonian. When I go to Rome, Italy I may want to check out a punk squat but I'll also want to see the Coliseum. Yes, I realize that my analogy fails in that it equates the great artifacts of Western Culture with that peculiar dance move wherein the rump vibrates as if hooked to high-voltage jumper cables, to which I can only respond: well, Western Culture, in the immortal words of Janet Jackson, "what have you done for me lately?"

So anyway: I'm gyrating suggestively on the dance floor of "the Bootie Barn" in Tampa, Florida, involved in this activity only on account of my pure social-scientific interest in observing indigenous Floridian culture, you understand—to my immediate left Jon Asher of the Red Scare is himself involved in a quite compelling approximation of high-voltage buttock wiring, causing nervous but not totally disapproving glances to cast in the general vicinity of the spacious area we've cleared for ourselves in the center of the dance floor with the aid of flailing, uncoordinated limbs. Jon turns to me suddenly, in mid-dance move, his face serious and somber.

"Man," he says, "that Y2K is some fucked up shit."

Notice how these thoughts always come to you at the most incongruous times? Did the ancient Romans, sitting in the stone bleachers of the Coliseum, being fed grapes by eunuch slaves as they drunkenly cheered a lion disemboweling some unfortunate gladiator, ever pause in mid-revelry to note that their empire was in decline? We create diversions to mask the unraveling of the social fabric; look at pre-fascist 1930's Germany, with its culture of extravagant denial, or the disco dancing which pre-figured Reagan in 1970's America. The difference between the fall of the Roman empire and the fall of the American empire, though, is that while drunkenly reveling at the Coliseum, your average Roman may have had some vague notion of barbarians amassing on the horizon, ready to one day sweep in and loot and pillage, but there was no set date for this ransacking. We, on the other hand, have constructed an elaborate doomsday clock for ourselves and set the alarm to go off at midnight, year 2000.

There's the crux: either the computers break down, leading to dance clubs being taken over by right-wing militias who convert the dance floors into military tribunals and stage kangaroo trials, executing all the weirdos with no survival skills to offer in the realms of hunting and gathering (Jon and I, with our barely passable bootie dances and rudimentary guitar playing abilities, do not make the grade); alternatively, the computers will not break down, in which case all this dance-while-ye-may-for-tomorrow-we-shall-die premised behavior is going to seem even more arbitrary and pointless than ever, and Western Civilization grinding and droning on in the fashion it seems to be grinding and droning on in lately, we'll all end up settling into our lives as office flunkies cruising internet chat rooms for the rest of eternity, or at least until the year 20,000. As long as a somewhat plausible argument exist for option A, though, it seems hard to argue for, well, anything really. The prospect of wide-scale technological and social breakdown seems to render all political discourse, long-term life planning, employment prospects, and most other non-foraging related topics null and void.

Of course, I could be looking pretty foolish telling you all to start preparing for the End if option B occurs and everything goes anticlimactically on as usual. However, I myself do not like or endorse the way things are going now, much as the alternatives also discomfort me. I don't want an office job, and the first long-term study of internet usage reveals the rather unsurprising evidence that it causes not only breakdowns in actual social support and friendship networks, but leads to increased feelings of alienation and disconnectedness from others in the user. Why not instead learn some useful survival skills? I've spent a good deal of time and energy building up a network of friends and compatriots in this little subculture of ours, and I'm going to be damn disappointed if the Road Warrior scenario goes down and none of you know how to build a campfire or which mushrooms are poisonous. On the other hand, if the system does survive intact into the twenty-first century, all of the things which are currently null and void—political discourse, long-term planning for the future, etc.—will be back in effect, and, having heaved our heavy sighs of relief that civilization is intact, we'll have to get back on task figuring out how to subvert and destroy it. In the meantime, though, as we await the crucial moment when the lights go out or don't, I recommend learning a few practical skills and otherwise making a concerted effort to have as good a time as you can before the foraging begins. Check out a museum, go to a dance club. Whatever you want your last moments to be.

ROME, 1984

I had my first experiences with anti-American sentiment in Rome, Italy, at the age of thirteen. At that time I was attending a predominantly German-language school. It was doubly weird, because not only was I in an unfamiliar locale, I was surrounded by German lads who, although in much the same boat as I was in terms of alienation from their surroundings, decided that at least they could find some commonality and group identity in tormenting and ostracizing the lone dorky American kid.

The thought of whether my country did or did not blow had never crossed my mind before, nor had the idea that this reflected on me as a citizen. I had never actually considered the fact that I was a citizen of somewhere, since my educational experience and social options had generally never involved being included in anything, from softball teams where I was chosen last and asked to display my genitals as proof that I was not a girl to lunatic paramilitary rednecks in my neighborhood who chased me around, threatening to beat me up for the sheer arrogance of deigning to exist. "You think you're cool," they'd jeer. "You think you're number one, don't ya?" I did think I was number one, but only out of one.

The concept of radical individualism manifested itself initially as self-evident to me, the inherent lesson to be learned from leaving the house every morning and noting how unique and strangely alone every person in the universe seemed to be, although when and where they were all meeting to band together and persecute me for my differences was unclear to me.

The German kids had some of their facts straight, though. I would bluster and pout when attacked and interrogated on subjects like gun control or treatment of the homeless, trying to retort with broad, sweeping statements cribbed from the lyrics of the national anthems and pledges of allegiance of my land, none of which I'd memorized or paid particular attention to. This made a coherent rebuttal difficult. I'd actually been kicked out of the cub scouts for refusing to memorize the pledge of allegiance, which I suppose I could now re-interpret as one of my first conscious acts of resistance to the status quo, but I can remember pretty clearly, if truth be told, that what was really going on back then was that this totally awesome television program called *Ultraman* (Japanese import, by the way) was filling my consciousness so completely that I didn't feel I had the time to clutter my brain with useless trivia when there were so many fantasy battles between gigantic rubber monsters to wage in my mind.

The Germans, and to a lesser extent the Italians, hassled me about my nationality, but in the end what saved me was the great universalizer, the English language. And not just any old sentences, bandied about like I owned the place (American and British tourists often make this mistake, thinking that worldwide fascination with English, be it through films, television, music, or English-speaking celebrities, is based primarily in the beauty and syntax of the language itself, and therefore their high-pitched nasal exhortations to "bring the check and make it snappy" will be received with the same jubilant cheer pop stars enjoy when shaking their rumps for audiences internationally). What saved me was, of course, my knowledge of swear words and sexual idiom, not to mention my close cultural ties with the Artist Then At The Time Still Known As Prince. This was the year that the film *Purple Rain* and accompanying soundtrack album appeared, becoming a huge smash hit in Italy, as well as all other countries where doing synchronized dances involving bird-flapping motions was not punishable by having your hands cut off in the public square. Chief among his smash successes in Italy was a song that at the time was considered quite nasty, entitled "Darling Nikki." Although English as a foreign language was a requisite part of my school's curriculum, and typically most western European students receive a working knowledge of at least some basic English, certain key phrases and concepts from this racy ballad were being omitted from the vocabulary lists we eighth graders were receiving. I found myself the sudden possessor of highly coveted and contraband information, or what in the parlance of rap lingo is called "street knowledge": I knew, for instance, the definition of the word "masturbate" and what it meant, exactly, to "grind."

There was no end to the youth who were fascinated by these lyrics. I was approached by a steady stream of them at recess every day. Former bullies, taunters, and evil eye-givers suddenly appeared before me, amiable and sometimes even slightly reverent, asking, "OK, he meets her in a hotel lobby, and she's, uh, from what I understand, doing something with a magazine but not reading it, exactly." I'd lay the knowledge on them. Clearly, their classmates had already relayed it to them, but somehow they just had to hear it from the horse's mouth, perhaps merely because the horse was located in such convenient proximity, did a fairly good Prince impersonation (if I do say so myself), and, probably not least important, repetition of these key phrases and concepts could only up the amount of swearing and lewdness being bandied about, which was what life was all about in Italian eighth grade, and I imagine in eighth grades the world round.

As an oracular vessel, transmitting the wisdom of the American superstars to the eager populace, I gained a strange sort of minor proxy celebrity myself. I can only be thankful that I grew up in relatively innocent times. I think, had the music of 2-Live Crew been presented to me I would have been taxed to my limit, probably having to admit after an exhaustive 72-hour marathon decoding sessions that I had no idea what he was referring to with "honkey hos at donkey shows" but that it was probably a reference to gardening implements being raffled at some sort of rodeo. In any case, Prince was not such a tough nut to crack, and Europeans, who "find it difficult to understand American culture except as a totality" (to quote my housemate, explaining to me recently why neon orange sweatpants make him look sophisticated and continental) did not seem to have a problem lumping me in with their hero; despite the fact that I was from North Carolina and wore ratty heavy metal T-shirts, I was still somehow the resident expert on the urban funky experience.

I utilized my position of prominence to become the arbitrator of taste and morality within the group of socially retarded boys that ended up congregating in my gravitational vicinity. This mostly involved my schooling them on getting drunk and stumbling through the streets of the city, a hobby I was cultivating at the time. We also went to the movies a lot, lots of American films, often in the original language—thirteen is a formative age in terms of cementing your ideas of what you consider hip and cool and establishing the foundations of some sort of social identity; to watch these kids slowly swell up, sponge-like, absorbing the messages and values of American culture, gave me a feeling of warmth and familiarity. I didn't know anything about the homeless situation or gun control, but I knew the myth, not as expressed in archaic folk hymns but the phantasmal and fascinating American fantasy world of car chases, candy bars, cowboys, comic books. To watch them become hypnotized by a version of this same myth made me feel that it was valid and real.

The experience was short-lived, and soon I was back in the good old U.S. of A., my brief tenure as culture Czar at an end, and forced back into my position as radical individualist loner with genitals of an indeterminate nature. Within the context of America, American culture just became culture, and the feeling of deep personal pride I felt when my classmates laughed themselves into convulsions at Eddie Murphy's witticisms in the film *48 Hours*, as if it reflected on me personally because I came from the same small neighborhood where Eddie and I were in fact neighbors and collaborated on comedy material all the time, faded into the realization that there were a lot of 7-11's, highways, educational facilities, barbed wire fences, and money separating me and Eddie. Here, in America, I was just another anonymous consumer, no greater or less for my knowledge of street lingo, and shocked when, my first day or two back in the states, I sauntered over to the refrigerator and helped myself to a beer.

"What do you think you're doing?" my dad asked.

"I'm going to get trashed and stumble around the streets," I shrugged.

"You're thirteen years old," my father replied, snatching the beverage from my hands.

"But—but I—" I was stunned. But there was no fighting the mores and constitutional by-laws of the land. That sort of behavior might be acceptable in Italia, but here in the U.S.A. I was suddenly a minor again, and I'd have to wait another seven years before I could take up my hobby with the full consent of the law. The scales began to peel back from my beady little eyes, and I saw what was really going on. I had been wrong; the Europeans who had taunted me had been right. America was not the paradise of freedom and scantily clad attractive people that the cinema and popular radio hits depicted it to be. It was a totalitarian hellhole where years of psychologically crushing high school would reward me only with a job at the gas station and, if I could hold out a few more years without purchasing an easily accessible and background check-free firearm with which to blow my own head off in despair, I might eventually be allowed the privilege of buying some of the cheap, ethanol-grade liquid which passed for beer here in this depraved land. Had the makers of Schlitz never heard of the *Reinheitsgebot* of 1412? You only needed four ingredients to make beer, but I supposed the added preservatives and taxidermy agents contained in cans of the available domestic swill were added to control the raging tumors and cancers I'd have by then from my years of breathing in gasoline fumes at my day job.

I was quite perturbed by these revelations. I made several attempts to phone my friends in Italy and warn them that I was a false prophet, to implore them to immediately cease attending matinee shows of brainwashing American propaganda films, and to throw off the yoke of tyranny being cast over them by repeated listenings of Prince and all the other radio crap which was poisoning their minds with the values of my evil land. Unfortunately, I could not figure out how to dial the country code.

SYNOPSIZER

The newest version of Microsoft Word features a nifty function called the synopsisizer (actually I have no idea what it's called, but it is a sweet feature regardless of the specifics), which allows you to speed-edit your writing, cutting out the chaff and poncey alliterations to broil it all down to the brine of the naked facts themselves so as to better deliver these bare-bones essentials to your business focus group or attention-deficit disordered child. Whatever text you insert, this synopsis function will give you, depending on your intensity of synopsisization, anything from the *Reader's Digest* version to what the dust jacket would say to what *TV Guide* would say and on down to the basic three words that most cogently sum it all up. There is some weird formula by which it functions, and I can't quite figure it out; although the first sentences of paragraphs tend to make good showings in the final edits, the machine will sometimes pick random bits from the middle or two-thirds of the way through, opting to display strange groupings of randomly assembled snippets as its final pronouncement on what you were really trying to say.

I've been trying it out on previous columns I've written, setting the synopsis function on "max." It's interesting to see what it all boils down to. One reduced itself to this curt summation:

"I've gotten two letters in my life which postulated the theory that I hate women. Hey, I'm an artist."

See? That's pretty good.

I am an artist. Oh, those are indicting words indeed. Aside from the fundamental logical flaw of ascribing inherent character traits to your propensity for making crafts (you believe that you behave in certain ways on account of your artisticness? As if it's got some sociobiological roots, being an artist more akin to being Albanian than to being a garbage man or an insurance claim adjuster), there is just the pure annoyingness of dealing with someone pompous and self-important enough to claim themselves as a part of this special breed (which apparently includes me, since I wrote the sentence, although looking through the original text there is so much chaff and digression that I can't find it. Maybe I accidentally hit the Microsoft smartass commentary function).

A cogent summation of my criticism of people with such notions of their own self-importance is to be found in the film *The Decline of Western Civilization Part Two: The Metal Years.* In the film, we get a montage of Axl Rose wannabe after Axl Rose wannabe, bedecked in what we can now, from our twenty-first century vantage point, see as grievous scarf-based offenses to fashion and general aesthetic taste, each delivering almost the exact same monologue, revolving around their own genius and the inevitability of their second-rate Guns N' Roses knock-off of a band "making it." "What if you don't make it? What then?" the interviewer asks. "What's your plan B?" The answers are uniform and chilling in the simplicity of their cretinism. "There is no plan B," each Axl asserts with stoic confidence. We can only imagine the sad fates which must have befallen these plan B-less unfortunates, fates which probably involved a lot of visits to the plasma center and to the salvation army to try selling scarves. And it is not the plan B-lessness per se which offends me—you should see my resumé—but the self-indulgences which this attitude permits the young Axls to allow themselves on account of their intense self-conviction. "Sure, I live off my girlfriend," they tell the camera. "She pays the rent, buys me food, scores me drugs. But it's cool, man, because she knows it's all coming back to her times ten when I make it. Limo rides, fur coats, a swimming pool in the shape of my genitals—I'm gonna pay her back with interest, man." Needless to say, these unfortunate women are still waiting for their pools.

I suppose, like most things that really enrage a person, I find the behavior of the protagonists of this documentary so particularly reprehensible because I can so clearly see myself reflected in them. I have no hopes of heavy metal superstardom, but I do have many hobbies and interests which provide disturbing parallels. For instance: like most people who spend a good deal of time involved in working on their "creative writing," I admittedly will spend about 30% of the time actually writing and the other 70% just sitting around and reflecting on how brilliant I am. William Faulkner wrote many of his greats while employed as the night watchman of a factory, totally blowing off his job and being fired for gross incompetence as a result. Of course, now that he's, you know, William Faulkner, it all seems funny and ironic, and they probably have a plaque up at the factory over a bronze typewriter, reading, "W. Faulkner wrote *As I Lay Dying* here," whereas the truth of the matter is most likely "W. Faulkner was told to pick up his shit and get the fuck out after being found asleep over his typewriter here." No doubt, had he been interviewed by a documentary film team after being fired, he would have said something along the lines of, "Hey, man, I am a literary genius. You should read my stuff. Man, I am one of the greats, and one day the world will recognize my writing prowess." "But you just lost your job," the documentarian would then ask. "What if your gamble doesn't pay off? What if you labor in obscurity and die forgotten? Any plan B?"

"Plan B?" Faulkner would have rightly scoffed. "There is no plan B."

Of course, rigid adherence to the formula (obsessive fixation on your own genius, coupled with an inability to hold down any job since the muse might call you to work at any moment), while it is worthwhile just because it will get you out of work, does not guarantee you next William Faulkner status. That's where Microsoft Word comes in: thanks to new, quality of life improving innovations like the synopsisizer, the whole literary genius bracket can now be standardized into obsolescence. Since I use archaic technology, my prose continues to follow the fruity conventions of olde English—however, on the occasions when I do get a crack at the more new-fangled Microsoft Word, I notice that the computer automatically underlines grammatically dicey sections in green.

"Spelling and grammar check" yields the root cause of my errors: "long sentence (no suggestions)." I take this lack of constructive criticism to indicate "beyond hope," but, apparently, the newest versions will actually go so far as to rewrite these sections for you. So what you end up reading is, technically, not the work of the credited author but the writing of the Microsoft Word computer program. An interesting development, in my mind—kind of points to the ramifications of the shift in our language from "writing" to "word processing." Soon enough, it should be possible to not only set levels for synopsisization and grammatical clarity, but for Faulknerization as well. We'll set our computers on "synopsisize at 30%" and "geniusize at 95%." Soap operas are already being written with programs that randomly generate plot, inserting amnesia or sudden appearance of long-lost twin brother in combinations which transfix audiences of millions, so even content shouldn't be hard to generate with the current available technology.

The new literature will be like the new music or the new art: easily produced by anyone according to mathematically generated formulas, quantized, pitch- and color-corrected. Talent is obsolete; now anyone who wants to invest in the software will be just as much of a genius as anyone else. Then it's just a matter of falling asleep in front of your monitor and getting fired from work.

PUNK OVER 30 / DEAD PUNKS

I missed the deadline for the "Punk over 30" issue, and I have no regrets about this. Being punk over thirty ain't shit, try being punk over forty. Try being punk over fifty: Joe Strummer couldn't manage it. The *Chicago Tribune*, reporting on his death a couple of days before Christmas, spells it out: Strummer, founding member of the Clash, "the greatest" and "most creative punk rock band," is dead at fifty. This is a deserved eulogy, but you have to wonder, what did Joe Strummer eat on a typical day for lunch? Was he a heavy smoker? Did he sleep on the floor a lot? And if a person of his stature can't make it physically past fifty, what is the life expectancy of the ramen noodle eating mid-thirties punks with no health insurance? Thirty-six?

Plans are underway to induct the Clash into the Rock 'n' Roll Hall of Fame; the Ramones, none of whom seem like they are going to make it past fifty-five, have already been inducted. A friend of mine was invited to their induction ceremony. "What do you wear to an event like that?" he wondered aloud days before. "Formal attire? Or leather jacket and bowl cut?" What would the surviving Ramones be wearing? Leather jacket and bowl cut would seem like the punk thing to do. But when you're being inducted into a hall of fame on account of your feats of punkness, has the point already been made bluntly enough? Is it time to just accept your iconic lot, put on a tuxedo, and start shaking people's hands?

"Punk's not dead, it just deserves to die," sang Jello Biafra, as far back as 1986. But he meant it as a figurative death: punk is now dying literally here on the mortal plane. We, the living, can choose to adopt the lifestyle known as "punk," but we'll never be "punk" in the same authorial way that Joe Strummer or Joey Ramone were. "Perhaps dedicated individuals still speak of the genuine, real thing," writes George Petros, "but in fact they choose a lifestyle demographic, just like jazz or blues or metal…. or sports or movies. It just keeps on going on; if ya dig it, it's cool." *If ya dig it, it's cool*—not exactly as compelling as *the only band that matters*.

It seems to me that, as lives go, Strummer's was a good one. He was a "success," "the greatest, most creative" punk rocker of his time. It was printed in the *Tribune*, and thus becomes historical record, to be microfiched and archived for later junior high school research paper usage. Billy Bragg, quoted in the *Tribune* article, says, "Without the Clash, the political edge of punk would have been severely dulled." But the paper hastens to point out that "despite uncompromising political principles, the Clash were commercially successful by punk standards." Uncompromising political principles and commercial success are not antithetical according to the principles of punk, apparently. That sort of thinking is the stoic ideological domain of hardcore punk, which recognizes that when Bragg talks about "political edge" he's talking about triple LPs dedicated to Nicaraguan revolutionary movements, not politics in the ordinary, what-are-you-going-to-buy-at-the-grocery-store way. DIY hardcore took the politics one step further. Crass mocked the Clash as major label sellouts and advocated living in communes and starting your own record label; from the vantage point of hardcore, punk rock was still just rock and, thus, as bankrupt as the culture it criticized. Hardcore was self-consuming; its rejection of everything left little room for anything. That's the nature of iconoclasm—it's a destructive force by definition, and, when there are no more idols to be smashed, there is nothing left to wreck but yourself. Biafra wasn't talking about punk when he said it deserved to die; he was talking about hardcore punk. That was the "stale cartoon" which punk had become by 1986, and it keeled over, seemingly on demand of its principal architect.

1986! I remember it, actually, but it was a long time ago. I'm certainly not thrilled to think that I'm involved in outmoded pursuits, just as the caretaker of a letterpress doesn't want to hear about how great laser printers are, but there are certain realities which must be faced by even the most creative anachronists among us. I'm not sure punk deserves to die, but Joe Strummer will attest that this does seem to be the forensic reality of the situation. We can gnash our teeth in nostalgic grief, or we can spit on his grave, and—like the bowl-cut vs. the tuxedo—it's hard to say which action would be the punker of the two. Strummer, at least, can rest in peace, knowing that what he created will live on, at least in some *Chicago Tribune*-digestible format. As for Biafra, who upped the ante for another generation of angry kids: if he was that disillusioned in 1986, I'd hate to hear what he has to say about his lawsuit-riddled legacy now. If punk was just rock and hardcore demanded more, that only makes the failure more profound. "If the music's gotten boring it's because of the people who want everything to sound the same," sang Biafra, and that's you, punks under 30, choosing a lifestyle demographic, your thing that "if ya dig it, it's cool," finding connectedness and comfort in something that was created in a spirit of divisiveness and discomfort. Punk wasn't enough for the people who came up with hardcore; why is it enough for you?

MARRIAGE

I'm hoping that I'll be one of the first to die, so that I don't have to go through the inevitable filling up of my calendar with funerals to attend, feeling left behind as everyone passes me up in line, as per usual, on the race to the finish. Then again, is there free food at funerals? I hate to miss even a tiny morsel of free food. I can well imagine that it will be promises of buffets, be they art openings, lectures, deaths, or just the rumor of some parade float later this afternoon handing out complimentary donuts, which will keep my heart beating its steady resolve, the will to live and live, if only to get my best value for the dollar on the hospital costs of being born.

I'm experiencing a sort of funereal foreshadowing in the current crop of marriages inundating my peer group these days. The inevitable march of time lays claim to another generation, and we see sociological trends repeated in the new batch of kids, inevitable as seasons, scientifically predictable as clockwork. In Chicago, marriage has replaced vests as the new trend amongst the late-twenty-somethings. I couldn't get into vests either. I jumped on the bandwagon initially, and procured one of these puffy, sleeveless garments, complete with garish color-scheme and racing stripe motif. But I found I couldn't hang; perhaps the paradoxical nature of a sleeveless winter garment was too much for my mind to bear, or perhaps it was the forward-thinking fashion sense of Andrew Dickson, who was rocking vests unapologetically while the other fashion plates scoffed and scoured the thrift stores for gas station jackets adorned with monogrammed monikers of all-American gas-pumpers like "Ed" or "Al" (how ironic to think of yourselves working at a gas station, fashion plates), which produced in me the uneasy feeling that I'd be biting his style.

My peers, essentially a pretty square bunch despite their exotic piercings and skateboard company logo tattoos, will, of course, follow the latest trends, and thus will probably all tie the knot by the time they reach their early thirties. Go ahead and get married, I don't mind; live and let live, I always say! But I know these people will not show the same level of toleration for my free-wheeling ways. I have a recurring fantasy of being that last unmarried guy in the extended social sphere of my acquaintances, and it is pretty grim, the thought of being invited over to some old friends' house for dinner, to sit at a long table, among rows of couples; I imagine myself seated at the head of the table, and the eager sets of four eyes turning to leer at me as someone goes, "So, how's the bachelor life?" I begin to explain how nice it is to have free time and how my model railroad is really coming along, but then I stop short because I notice, seated at the other end of the table, the only remaining unmarried woman, shifting and squirming in her seat just as uncomfortably as I will be, with everyone nudging us and poking our ribs and rolling their eyes in the direction of the other end of the table.

People! Let me explain to you, yet again, the difference between a model railroad and an actual, living human. Should the various socialization errors incurred in childhood cause me to feel the need to tie a model conductor to the tracks and allow him to be beheaded by a speeding train every once in a blue moon, that is all right. It's not hurting anybody. This friend of yours, this only remaining unmarried woman, Irma or whatever you said her name was, she seems a fine, decent woman; it's not her fault that she isn't married. Don't punish her further by setting her up with me.

I don't imagine that I will ever get married. What's the point? Fifty percent of marriages end in divorce. Why should I be so optimistic as to think I can beat the odds? Even amongst the happily married, you find that a good percentage of those people are miserable, too. The rarest of couplings may produce a union of blissful matrimony; even my short-term relations tend to end in head-wounds. The bachelor life seems my inevitable lot. Still, I'm happy to attend: weddings, involving extensive catering and usually no corpse, are a more upbeat circuit for getting snacks than funerals.

•　　　•　　　•

My stepsister Sarah has recently decided to marry for the second time, presumably calculating that at 50% divorce rates, her second marriage is statistically guaranteed to work out. I make some calculations of my own and procure the next available plane ticket to North Carolina to attend the occasion. Surprisingly, my showing up for the wedding seems to be interpreted as a touching gesture;

various family members make a point of expressing to me how nice it is of me to make the time, expend the effort, how much it means to my sister, and so on. This all makes me feel a little guilty, of course; my maturity and adult propriety are praised, and I find myself being treated as an exemplary family member—meanwhile, I have the whole thing mathed out in my head, an undeniable equation: the plane ticket is $100, but between the wedding and associated family dinners, I can easily consume $300 of food, equaling $200 profit I stand to gain by going to this wedding. All these years and the family still has not accepted my fundamental living orientation, and now my scavenging is even reinterpreted as sentimentality.

Each time Sarah enters a new phase of her life I realize how much I'll miss the old Sarah: I missed the collegiate partyer of her early twenties when she got married for the first time, I missed her persona as the black sheep of family drama (and how she made me look innocuous and stable, contextually) when her marriage settled into normalcy and routine after getting off to a great start as a scandalous affair involving breaches of international law, exorbitant payments to South American government officials, visas and green cards, as well as my stepsister's brief tenure as an employee of Pizza Hut. And now, I realize, I'll miss her newest incarnation, the twenty-four year old divorcée, who lamented to me about the tribulations of post-marital living, the difficulty of getting back into the singles scene, the complex legal wranglings of separation, all making me feel like I was talking to someone much older than me, and I'll miss the pleasant temporal dislocation I'd feel when it suddenly occurred to me that this person, with their strange adult concerns, was actually several years younger than me. One day, perhaps she'll have children, and I'll attend birthday parties, seated at the children's table, a forty year old man with frosting on my face. In Chicago, it's easy to pull off this look: I can hide in the eternal wayward youth of being a new face among an essentially interchangeable set of snapshot faces, ahistorical and identifiable only by my allegiances of the moment, a 90 Day Men pin on my gas station jacket, a photo-mat strip in my pocket of myself with some people whose names I won't know in a week. In Carrboro, time moves differently, it's all continuum and continuity. I come back here to find my friends have married, own houses, have children. The children are entirely different beings from visit to visit; they go from embryonic to speaking to having fashion sense and taste in music. It's shocking at first, and then it becomes placating, almost comforting in an odd way. I have to admit to a certain sense of relief in seeing all of this happen, in watching my generation step up to bat. It's nice to realize that we are not that much sketchier than our parents. We are not the dismal failures I thought we'd be; we are as capable as any generation before us of replicating the social institutions that keep our civilization intact.

At a PTA thrift store, I buy a suit. "Family function," I tell the lady behind the counter. "A happy one, I hope," she replies. "It all depends on how you look at it," I say. *Family function* is actually a good phrase for it, since it sounds sort of gastrointestinal, or like a euphemism for purely procreational sex. I imagine the first wedding is where you pull out all the stops, romance-euphemism-wise. Your first wedding is probably more easily interpreted as an event outside the contexts of history and temporality, beautiful in and of itself, the proverbial "happily ever after," which you accept as a small child and find yourself questioning when you begin to understand the mechanics of time and entropy. By the second wedding the fairy tale factor has diminished considerably, and the whole thing becomes way more family functional. Sarah tells me that her fiancé proposed to her in the car on the way to Home Depot. "The ring's in the glove box," he had said, pointing. Not exactly Prince Charming behavior, but on the plus side, no hostage airlifts or international diplomacy involved, and I guess that's what she's going for this time around.

It's hard not to extrapolate funeral from wedding, somehow, and, like some form of unintentional free-association, we keep referencing them inadvertently. We get caught in traffic on our way to the wedding, and my brother comments that our caravan of cars should have gotten funeral tags so that we could avoid the traffic. I decide to reveal to my parents my wishes for my own burial. "I want to be lowered into the ground while a huge PA blasts 'Another One Bites the Dust,' by Queen," I say. Her mind currently preoccupied with the finances of family functions, my stepmom's immediate response to the request is, "Well, casket burials are pretty expensive. Cremation is more economical. Could we just scatter your ashes to 'Another One Bites the Dust?'"

The wedding takes place in a small rented hall in Greensboro, North Carolina. I have never met the groom, and it's a shock to all of a sudden be in a room full of his extended relatives.

I am introduced to one garishly tuxedoed uncle after another, a seemingly endless cavalcade of cousins and old football buddies, and worse, the unmarried daughters, buffed, polished and painted up like overripe fruit priced to sell. "Isn't it romantic?" says one young lady in a recycled prom-dress, pointing across the room to where Sarah stands in full bridal getup, meeting and greeting with the glazed perma-grin you only see on brides and people who are on court-mandated tranquilizers.

"Sarah looks pretty killer," I reply. "That's a nice dress. I think, personally, that she should have gone a little more goth with it. A little black lipstick, some of those Marilyn Manson contact lenses that give you goat pupils—now, that would be a bride!"

Looking around the room, I feel bad for my new in-laws. Here we are, in full force, the Burian-Highs: between the PTA suits, weird affects, and continental accents, we're like the cast of *Fawlty Towers* crossed with the staff of a crystal meth lab. If I were them, I wouldn't want to marry us. But it's too late now, the ritual has begun: "This marriage joins together these two families and creates a new one," says the minister, gesturing around the roomful of people squirming at precisely that prospect. Familial union, the joining together of tribes, a corporate merger of conglomerates dedicated to no more lofty a goal than the reproduction of ourselves, more of us, crowding the world with our pointless puttering. The rivers of our lives flow together, creating a new river, and, between the assembled Burians, the Highs, and now these new people whose name I didn't catch, that's a pretty sketchy damn river.

Rings fetched from glove compartments and exchanged, permission given to kiss the bride, bride kissed, the marriage is consummated, and it's finally time for the main event: the food and beverages are served. My elbowing and pushing at the buffet table causes the already skeptical unmarried belles to erase me as a prospect. Frances, my younger stepsister, is sidled up along next me at the trough-line, and I ask her opinion on the grand union. "What do you think of our family versus their family?" I ask. She looks across the room, assesses the other side. "Well, there's more of us," she notes, matter-of-factly, seeming to imply that if it ends up coming down to hand-to-hand combat, we could overpower them.

Champagne is served. The father of the groom stands up to make a toast. He is an imposing figure, a giant man with a scraggly grey beard, his bulky frame stuffed awkwardly into a suit which probably cost him more than my salvation army standard issue, but which he will probably wear just as infrequently. The room goes silent, and I register an air of trepidation on the other side of the room, as if it is commonly understood within the family rank and file that big poppa is not a man to mince words, that he is the kind of guy who might actually stand up and object at a wedding or blurt out, "I never liked that sum'bitch anyway!" at a funeral. Tension fills the air as he collects his thoughts.

"Well, I'm the *father* of the groom," he growls sternly. "And this *ain't* the first time I've seen him married." Low groans emanate from the corners of the room, silenced as his steely gaze sweeps the hall, daring someone to step up to him, challenging someone to tell the father of the groom to hush, that this is a sacred, fairy tale moment. Then his eyes go soft, and he looks back at his son. "This ain't the first time I've seen him married," he repeats and smiles. "But it's the first time I've seen him happy." *Aaawwws* fill the room. "And if they're happy, well," he looks over at our side of the room, "I reckon that's all that really matters."

If they're happy that's all that really matters. I suppose that is true. But will they live happily ever after? Will we all become a prosperous conglomerate together? At that moment I see that it doesn't really matter. No one is asking for that. No one is expecting it. The ring is in the glove box, and the wedding has the funeral implicit in it—"till death do us part" is the best case scenario. This family function is a happy one, and happy occasions are few and far between, and they are never the last stop. They are just one more rung on the ladder down into the earth as "Another One Bites the Dust" cranks over the PA. The father of the groom is right on, I think. It's too easy to be cynical. It seems OK to accept that this is a meaningful moment, to accept the inevitable passage of time, to come to grips with it, embrace the present and go back to the buffet table for more tortellini. I think I understand, now, in some way, what draws people into marriage. A wedding is not about permanence at all; it's about seizing a moment. Maybe it's a wish: a way of saying, publicly, "Look at this, we're happy, this is a rare thing, we wish it would go on forever." Who knows? Maybe it will. I give them 50/50 odds. Still, here, suspended in the moment, in her wedding dress and with the assemblage of new in-laws surrounding her, I think to myself, Sarah looks happy, and that's great, that makes me happy.

HOME IN THE CITY

"Home in the city," as the Blue Oyster Cult puts it in their song "Burning for You," "isn't home to me." Indeed. "Home is the highway," sings Eric Bloom, soulfully interpreting the lyrics of music critic and fringe cultural icon Richard Meltzer, the proverbial fifth Beatle of the Blue Oyster Cult, a man I've met on one occasion and interpreted, falsely, as insane. Further research reveals the fact that Meltzer was, indeed, a satellite member of one of arena rock's shining luminaries of the 1970's, one of the various facts about his life which festers in his brain, producing angry and resentful bile which he can only vent by monologuing about how the world has conspired to keep him down. The version of Blue Oyster Cult's "Burning for You" which I have on a mixtape in the car right now is from their career high-point, *Extraterrestrial Live*, and during the breakdown part of some song from that album, poor E. Bloom, drunk on the magic of the moment, gloats into the microphone, "Well, well, well—here we are at the Poughkeepsie, New York, SOLD OUT TO THE MAXIMUM!!!" It's the mid-70s, the Ramones are just starting out, playing to fifteen angry kids in a dingy bar a few miles away from the sold out arena, Eric Bloom is gloating and the crowd goes wild; three or four years ago I heard that the BOC's nightly guarantee is low enough these days that it would almost be feasible to get them to play my house and pass a hat. It seems like that ought to soothe Meltzer's ire somewhat; after all, he still receives the occasional royalty check for penning the lyrics to a classic rock radio staple or two, while the band has to go out and suffer through the indignity of playing. The other great thorn in Meltzer's craw, Lester Bangs, the historically canonized creator of modern rock journalism (this canonization effectively serving to exclude Meltzer, who was right there, writing for the same damn magazines in the late sixties, getting whacked out of his skull with Led Zeppelin and Black Sabbath and Lester Bangs backstage, but now receiving none of the credit for blueprinting a lifestyle which has wrecked the lives of countless thousands) is long dead, killed by the very rock' n' roll excesses he articulated into literary existence during a very rock 'n' roll life, and Meltzer, always the bridesmaid and never the bride, lives out his life in an innocuous and anonymous little house in Portland, Oregon, where he awaits the arrival of anyone with an interest in the myriad of subjects he is qualified to complain about.

"Home is the highway—" It's difficult to get a really powerful and anthemic midlife crisis going when you've got seethers like Richard Meltzer cluttering up your archetypes of existence file. I'm working on it, and in the same way I try to visualize the Blue Oyster Cult bravely refusing to fear the reaper at some Elks Lodge in Long Island where thirty or so drunk hairspray casualties beer bong from pitchers of Miller Genuine Draft and play pool, Eric Bloom's voice cracking with that quiver of sublimated defeat as he says, "Port Jefferson Elks Lodge.... here we are.... at seventy-five percent of the fire marshal's legal capacity!!!" But I just can't help listening to the band and visualizing the arena, the lighters, the fifty-foot mechanized creature who shambles on stage and breathes fire during "Godzilla."

I have never sold out an arena, $200 is still the outer reaches of financial victory as far as playing a show is concerned, and sure, I'm no Eric Bloom, but I'm no Richard Meltzer either. "Burning for You," a power-ballad about rock 'n' roll and long-distance love, might ring with a bitter, ironic inverted meaning to Meltzer, who has burned brightly and now has the ashes in his mouth to prove it. I suppose there should be some sadness in it for me, too: home in the city is not home to me. I recognize that feeling in myself after even a brief trip away. Returning to the alien Chicago apartment, to the familiarity of the crack dealers in the alley, the same sad friends at the same sad bar, the clutter of my filing cabinet and stereo and all the other objects which are supposed to embrace you with their sense of comforting stability and nestedness—this might as well be the moon, I might as well be the weird, almond-eyed alien on the cover of the Blue Oyster Cult album, descending from the glowing craft and back into my own extraterrestrial life.

I'm burning for all kinds of people, places, and things these days. I have a romanticized and romantic attachment to geography—I fall in love with my surroundings, carry out tormented affairs with the landscape and architecture, have my heart broken eventually by everything and everyone. Like any break-up, you move on. Who can begrudge the curmudgeons of this world becoming bitter, resentful, begrudging? As the great innovators of rock journalism will not hesitate to show you, will not hesitate to scream at you from their front porches on a beautiful morning in Portland, Oregon: the more past you accrue, the more past there is to get stuck in. When I visit Portland now, it's like visiting an old girlfriend, seeing the familiar and yet somehow disconcertingly alien face of someone you used to be in love with, someone who was your world. On a beautiful day in Portland, when people comment offhandedly about how nice the place is, I protest, I tell them not to be fooled by her looks, you should see what she's really like, you should see her after it's been raining for days in a row, and the mascara has run, exposing the pale, sad eyes. You should feel how cold and clammy Portland can be. Oh, it's unfair, I know—Portland is not all cold and clam, but how can I allow myself to think otherwise? How can I face up to how I might have fucked up, what I might be missing out on?

I move a lot. My twenties, in a nutshell, can be summed up as a series of brief and unresolved interactions with people, bookended by long drives in vans of varying mechanical and bodily soundness. The motion and transience comforts me. It's what I'm used to. At twenty-seven it occurred to me that, no matter what I did with the next three years of my life, even were I to renounce rock music and get a job at the library or convert to some random and sedentary religious affiliation, it was too late: the die had been cast. The twenties would forever exist in my history as the van years, the decade I spent in transit, between places, unable to actualize or consummate, only to suggest and extrapolate.

You can't help but get callused emotionally by such behavior. Eventually you've familiarized yourself with the process of dis- and re-engaging, and, once you get the basic gist, it's just a matter of going through the motions. There comes that inevitable process of reinterpretation every time you start over in a new place—a recontextualization of your experience so that you can deal with the loss. You decide to focus on the bad times you've left behind: North Carolina, you're so hot and sultry, and it's hard to deny your looks, but when's the last time you offered to do my laundry? When's the last time you took me out to eat or to the movies? North Carolina, the romance is gone—you were cool at first, but after a while I felt I lost you, I was holding on to some imaginary way it could have been while you were coming home later and later, smelling like cigarettes and booze, muttering, "Oh, nowhere," when I'd ask where you'd been. Anyway, I'm in Chicago now—home in the city—and, as I go to sleep to gunshots and the whistling bird calls of street gang signals outside, it makes sense not to think about the nice days or the long walks, all the good times you showed me.

Home in the city: everyone knows I'm faking it. A geographical serial monogamist, every time I set up my filing cabinet and take my record collection out of some van, put it in some room somewhere, and boldly proclaim that I'm burning for this new romantic entanglement with a grid system of streets, public transit, and food stamp offices, when I make a grand gesture of sentiment—get a library card, for instance—the Meltzers of the world just roll their eyes. I have a surface and cursory knowledge of many places and social groups and individuals, but to answer the question of where I've *lived*—honestly?—I have to concede that I've only existed in most of these places, my body was there but I never full-on lived except in those brief moments when my stuff was back in storage and I was at a party half-drunk and trying to give away my library card to someone who might actually use it, the moment of weightlessness between places, waiting to get to the next place. There's a lesson to be learned from all of this, but it seems like I probably could have saved myself a lot of trouble and heartbreak by just learning that lesson from the lyrics to Blue Oyster Cult songs.

Still, "Burning for You" doesn't register to me as an admission of my personal, human failure; it's an anthem of victory, somehow, and not defeat. It's Meltzer's articulation of a lifestyle, a way of living, a stream of consciousness. Punk rock is just the latest attempt at expressing the inexpressible, an inadequate label to cling to, to define us and give us some sense that our self-destructive and antisocial activities have meaning and exist in a larger framework of greater importance than just us individually. The truth is simultaneously so much more and so much less: punk rock is nothing, a meaningless consumer-preference bracket that allows the mainstream culture to eventually produce lines of clothing and specialty record stores for you until what once was pure energy and excitement—what was once Blue Oyster

Cult in the early seventies—becomes a pathetic self-parody. But somewhere within that there are things which have real meaning, too, a historically continuous and much deeper, more subversive thread than any existing label or cultural categorization can express. You just have to keep moving, throw away what you can't carry with you, and store the things which you value enough that you can't slough them off. Meltzer is bitter, maybe, because he's seen the other world, where the transcendental moment can justify everything, and yet he's marooned here with the normal humans and their normal lukewarm concerns. I know how that feels. But you just keep moving.

RESIGNATION

Christ on a crutch, people! I've just received the newest issue of this magazine, and there on page three under the heading "cen-sor-ship," Mr. Kent McClard informs us that a certain Ravi Grover's column has been deleted from the pages of the very publication now besooting my sweaty little hands! Further, McClard informs us that the reason for this censoring is that Grover's expressed viewpoints are "diametrically opposed to the fundamental ideas of *HeartattaCk*." "This magazine has no obligation to provide him with space and you won't be reading his column in these pages," states Kent.

Reading those words, I am angered and outraged in a profound, almost inexpressible way. My column in the exact same issue is about Blue Oyster Cult! Further, during a tenuous analogy, I imply that I am unsatisfied with a former girlfriend for not doing my laundry regularly! How much more diametrical can you get!

Why does Ravi Grover get to be censored by *HeartattaCk* and Al Burian can't get his name out of print to save his life?

It's unfair. Since being knighted to the ranks of columnist during a secret ceremony in the back room of the Ebullition offices on that humid summer night back in the old millennium, my columnistic mission has always been to outrage the frumps at HC HQ, and, in all sincerity, I feel like I've put in some fine efforts. I've taken great pains to make only major label cultural references, endorse only bands that smoke pot, and suggest to the women of the world that they should perform acts of mass ritual murder against people like me and/or do my laundry if they have any free time.

That seems pretty censorable, doesn't it? The kind of thing which might get you kicked out of a reputable punk magazine filled with what Scott O' Neil, resigning from hardcore in a teary farewell letter in that same issue, describes as "fucking boring people that take everything so seriously." And yet, try as I might, not a peep from the reigning Czars of taste and decency. I've been turning in column after column, each time crossing my fingers and eagerly anticipating the torrent of indignation to be emailed back to me. But never have I received even the slightest protest. Not even a complaint about me in the letters section!

And then, to add insult to injury, this Ravi Grover character blasts past me in the fast lane on the superhighway of seditious thought, not only having his column banned but even getting a full explanatory write-up on the limits of first amendment protection printed in response to the unacceptable expression of whatever vile train of demonology he's found to spew! What could he possibly have come up with that could be so offensive as to overshadow my efforts?

Well, I'll confess that my immediate impulse here was one I've acted on a few times before, although I'm usually being paid at least $6.25 an hour when I do: "OK. If they won't fire me, I'll quit." I could probably get a gig over at *Maximumrocknroll*, and I bet I'd be in and out in one issue. Hell, I bet they won't even accept my first column (it'll probably be about interior decoration).

But then, what if they did accept my columns? What if I couldn't even get kicked out of *Maximumrocknroll*, a magazine with a stated editorial policy of excluding all things that aren't punk? In an almost oedipal way, can I deal with the implications of managing to slip an article on the Blue Oyster Cult into their "pioneers of punk" section?

McClard's point is well taken: his own censure from the pages of *MRR* for liking music which was, basically, too wimpy or too musically complex to fall in that magazine's range of coverage did not, after all, elicit in him the desire to produce a magazine which was all about freedom and the exchange of ideas in their multispectral glory; it made him start a publication based around his own tastes in music and its associated subculture. There are magazines out there for and about people who enjoy covering their entire bodies in non-porous materials, and these magazines have no obligation to cover non-rubberism-related topics, or, for that matter, to include counterpoint arguments against rubberism for balance. That's not censorship, that's just keeping things down to a manageable information level.

McClard's advice to Ravi and his compatriot gripers is the old "move west" argument, the publishing equivalent of advising the Mormons, "Hey, Utah is available." The outcasts are advised to start their own cultural production around the new subculture they've smithed. "Start your own magazine," he counsels. Hmmm, maybe I should do just that. What are we going to call this new subculture, though? *Fucking exciting people who take nothing seriously?* Well, it would probably have a higher circulation than a magazine named after having a coronary.

PART
THREE

Q: HOW'S YOUR SKELETON?
A: NOT SO GOOD!

Writing for the SKELETON NEWSPAPER

DR. PAZMINSKI, CHIROPRACTOR

When I moved to Chicago I could still, technically, count myself in the category of "young person." But now, six years later, things are different. At thirty-five, I am middle aged. I don't mean this to sound self-conscious or self-effacing—no, I am simply doing the obvious and inescapable math. Thirty-five is, if not squarely in the middle, at least the gateway into that range of numbers where, multiplied by two, you come up with a reasonable age to die. Push your designation of middle age much further forward, and you quickly get into the kinds of numbers that would seem an uncomfortable overstay, at least for the kind of life I'm attempting to lead.

Middle age has its advantages—you've settled yourself in, you've explored your abilities and limitations, and, having gained a sense of those parameters, you can relax a little. But, on the other hand, you have a real and distinct disadvantage in that, no matter how well things are going and no matter how gracefully you've matured into artistic or social self-confidence, none of that really matters at all, because the fact of the matter is that your body is now falling apart. As a young person, I managed to buck the trends—raves, grunge, newfangled appliances—but here, at last, I'm on the bandwagon. There is the dull, merciless pulse of the big wind-down all throughout my body. The bones ache, the skeleton itself is becoming rusty piping, popping and cracking, creaking and corroding.

Dr. Pazminski, whose chiropractic office I've been visiting with alarming frequency, does his adjustments and reconfigurations, like an accountant trying to re-work the math, up and down the abacus of the spine, coming up again and again with the same zero sum. He then gives me all the advice I don't want to hear. "You're too old to do heavy lifting!" he tells me point blank. "What do you eat? Are you vegetarian?" he frowns, shakes his head. "You're not *vegan*, are you?"

Pazminski brings a human pelvis into the office one day, holds it up for me to examine. "Bones don't decay outside of the body," he tells me. "This person died years ago, and look: the pelvis is undeteriorated. But when the bones are inside the body, they crumble and fall apart. Why do you think that is?"

"I don't know—corrosive bodily fluids?" I guess.

"I think it's the hate, fear, and anger we hold inside," Dr. Paz suggests. "It's the unresolved emotions, kept bottled up in our bodies, that dissolve us."

Hate? Fear? Anger? Who, me? Well, yes, OK: on the bus ride home from the chiropractor's office, a man screams at a woman in a wheelchair because her foot touched his clothes. "These shoes ain't cheap! I WORK for a living!" he berates her, as if the wheelchair is a sign of her sloth, a lifestyle accessory for laziness.

Meanwhile, a busload of people, myself included, sit there silently and passively, staring straight ahead, not intervening, doing our calloused city-dweller routine, pretending this isn't happening. It occurs to me that, hmm, yeah, maybe there is a little of all of that stuff being bottled up and pushed down into us, out here in the everyday. Maybe we do carry these unresolved interactions with us in our bodies, and maybe they really do go straight to the bones.

In any case, I really can't complain: I got the body I deserved, and I'm not a healthy liver. I've been blessed, but perhaps long-term cursed, with a strong and resilient constitution (about a +9, for you gamers). This has allowed me to generally act the fool for most of my life without serious or noticeable consequences. But, as time marches on, acting like a young person gets harder and harder to pull off. I don't bounce back as easily as I once did. It's harder to stay up all night, and my hangovers last longer. These are the typical excuses of my age bracket for watching some television and turning in at nine; in my case, though, I've simply plowed ahead with the youth mayhem lifestyle, having not modified my behavior significantly since 14, 24, or 34. I wonder at times if this is idiocy, and what exactly I have to show for it all, but then I remember: it doesn't fucking matter, it's too late, the long slow ride downhill for the body has begun. Faced with that central fact, who cares how good your drawings are? How symmetrical your face is? What tax bracket you're in? Pazminski is right: got to exercise more, drink less, eat enough protein. Other than that, who cares? No one path offers a better solution than any other for keeping anger, fear, jealousy, and pain out of your life. It's a good idea to focus on keeping yourself free of these things, on being a spiritual being, making yourself a vessel of hope and joy. But, like Pazminski's exercise sheets, it's a lot of effort and guaranteed not to work out in the end. You enter the battle to preserve your body knowing you are going to lose.

Yes, still listening to Iron Maiden here. Is this good or bad? Tradition, familiarity, continuity, or rut? How will it feel, when I am an old man laying on my deathbed, to think that I'm listening to this album for the last time? Will I feel foolish? Will I rue having squandered my time? Or will it cause me, even in those final moments, to spring from my bed, stand on a chair, and pump my fist in the air, crackling with a feeling of total triumphant victory?

Tonight, at the bottom of the well life-wise, I've put on *Piece of Mind* out of habit and turned it up out of spite. I had no intention of enjoyment. But, as the record begins, I find that I can't help myself. My mood goes from zero to ten in the space of Nicko McBrain's first awesome drum fill, and then there I am, smiling, air-guitaring, doing karate kicks, laughing at how good it all is. The lyrical themes are so positive: *fly on your way like an eagle, go where eagles dare, die with your boots on.* How can I criticize something that has so consistently been there for me in life, that has proven itself, time and again, so adept at providing that most elusive of feelings, a feeling that I've always heard you could get but have never been able to achieve with cocaine or crystal meth: raging, raving euphoria. *Bind all of us together! Ablaze with hope and free!*

Side A flies by flawlessly, but then I begin to get depressed and dissatisfied again. There are just too many problems: beginning with the album title, a second-rate pun. Who thought this was a good idea? Then there is the grotesque album cover, featuring band mascot Eddie in a state of raving insanity, head shorn bald, blood trickling from a large metal bolt screwed into his forehead. Not too subtle. There is the backwards message, obligatory for metal bands in 1983 (I went to the effort to play it forwards and hear what they were saying, years ago, but I can't remember what it was exactly—I think it was something about beer). And then there is the nadir in the middle of side B: "Quest for Fire," the worst Iron Maiden song ever. "In a time when dinosaurs walked the earth/when the land was swamp and caves were home/in an age when prize possession was fire/ to search for landscapes men would roam," sings Bruce Dickinson in his highest falsetto screech, blowing the whole possibility of mystical transcendence out of the water. A song about cavemen hanging out with dinosaurs? How can a record be so heavy one minute and so goofy the next?

You cannot choose your fate, and you cannot decide what things in your life will end up being important and meaningful to you. All you can do is accept the meaning. Here, nearing the anniversary of my ten millionth listening-to-*Piece of Mind*-while-contemplating-the-horror-and-futility-of-my-own-life, as "Quest for Fire" lurches into its absurd castrato-cadenced narrative, I find myself laughing. I finally get the joke. Instead of rushing over to skip the song, trying to cover the blemish, erase their mistake, I can finally just accept it: the song is fucking funny. The dumb humor is just as integral to the record as is its darkness, its transcendent positivity, and the musical awesomeness of the guitar solos. If I can embrace the whole, the totality of all its aspects, I might arrive at what Nietzsche called "a Dionysian Yes, the world as it is, without deduction, exception and selection." To achieve this is to joyously surrender, to love your fate and let all things be what they are. Here is the greatest heavy metal band of all time, at the apex of their abilities, fulfilling every cliché of the genre, even inventing a few new ones, kicking out some great jams and laughing their asses off while doing it. It is the distillation of the will to live and love living, and you can criticize it, resist it, or you could just go ahead and love it if you want to.

S tanding by the I-5 on-ramp, somewhere in rural northeastern Washington state, thumb extended, watching cars go by, Sunday afternoon. Monster trucks circle the block slowly, and new American cars, Ford Tauruses and Geos and what-not, purchased on credit by sad-eyed logging families who can't afford them, who only know that going further into debt is somehow giving them better credit. The new cars contain God-fearing people, patriotic people (as evidenced by American Flag decals on bumpers); I find myself thinking about Nathaniel Hawthorne's *Scarlet Letter*, the days of burning witches at stakes. You don't really think of America in Nathaniel Hawthorne terms much anymore. America is all Microsoft and cell phones and reality TV shows now, or so America would have you believe. Not here though; out here there are no internet cafés and there's not even enough going on that you could film a decent episode of *Cops*.

That is, until the townspeople band together to kill me, I imagine grimly as I catch another snarl of disgust flashed in return to my direct eye contact and earnest smile. You have to smile like that when you hitchhike, you have to project affability and pickupableness, but an hour of staring these people down, smiling and looking them in the eye and receiving looks of revulsion such that you feel as though you've smeared shit across your front teeth and are running a kissing booth by the I-5 on-ramp, that's demoralizing, and it is hard to maintain a sunny disposition and fully erect thumb under such conditions, hard to keep the shit-stained grin pearly and pickupable as rain clouds percolate overhead and the sky goes dark with night.

Eternal return! Because I've been in this exact situation before: in Bavaria, a place with proportionally about as many white supremacist enclaves in the hills as rural Washington, on a desolate highway on-ramp near no town in particular, trying to hitch my way to civilization on what turned out to be a religious holiday. Here, in the part of the world where Germans most closely resemble the cultural stereotypes of them presented in Europe-themed amusement parks in the U.S. and Japan (I'm talking lederhosen, beer steins, continued conviction that national socialism was great times), standing by the on-ramp as carloads of people dressed in their Sunday best and staring stonily ahead passed me by, I awaited uneasily the certain doom that was sure to befall me, for night to fall and the inevitable truckload of brown-shirted Bavarian teenagers to come upon me and pummel me into a fine, pasty, pudding-like consistency.

As I was resigning myself to the certainty of it, a sports car screeched off the highway, doing a dramatic U-turn in front of my eyes and screaming to a stop in front of me. "Get in!" the driver, an Italian guy wearing heavy gold chains, barked commandingly. I complied and we were off, racing through winding back roads at speeds which my lack of kilometric conversion ability thankfully prevented me from deciphering. The driver was an engaging, amiable guy, offering to converse in Italian, German or English—"Whatever you want, whatever makes you comfortable," he said cordially, screaming over the blaring Bee Gees CD in a rapid-fire Germano-English-Italian hybrid. Moments later, he abruptly ejected the Bee Gees, flinging the CD over his head and out of the sun roof in one fluid and graceful gesture. "Had enough of that," he muttered. The Bee Gees CD, it turned out, had been on repeat for the entirety of the forty-eight hours he'd been awake and driving at maniacal speed. Five minutes more of his non-stop, trilingual freestyling revealed him to be a cocaine dealer on his way to Frankfurt to transact a deal. "You seem like a pretty good guy," he told me, and offered to take me there and cut me in on it. I declined politely.

Back in eastern Washington, remembering all of this is heartening. What a great guy! And oh, what I wouldn't give for a suave Italian drug dealer to come screeching up right now. Anything, really, to deliver me from the clutches of the eastern Washington monster trucks, the mini-vans filled with tired women and their web-fingered offspring, whose unblinking fish-eye stares remind me of the hybrid children watching the sea in Metallica's "The Thing That Should Not Be." If these Washington state Bavaromericans are the new Hawthornian ideal, the cutting edge of virtuous puritan living, give me a drug dealer, a Satanist, a serial killer in an El Camino. Give me someone I can relate to. If the generally accepted cultural norms of "good" and "evil" are correct, why is it that the sketchballs, the social undesirables, the circus people and tax evaders, are the people who pick up hitchhikers? Why are the most obviously morally deficient elements of society also the most likely to display faith in the probability of human decency?

Then again, who am I to criticize the upstanding citizenry from the vantage point of desperately trying to thumb my way out of their town? I concede that, here by the highway, I must be blazing like a supernova, my whole appearance must be an affront to community standards and moral decency, a glimpse into some sort of obscure psychic credit of pure irresponsibility, a no-money-down automatic perfect credit rating with the universe which allows me to flaunt my homeless, jobless, morally relativistic, atheist communist free-love free-ride mentality like it's the newest fashion accessory from France. It seems pretty fair that they hate me, and, just as I'm wondering which is worse Bavaromerican brownshirts or faux-bohemian freeloaders, a car pulls over and a young kid blaring Christian emo from his Toyota hatchback swings open the passenger door, and it's on.

AL BURIAN IS A WRITER, ARTIST AND MUSICIAN. HE LIVES IN BERLIN, GERMANY. HIS PUBLICATIONS INCLUDE BURN COLLECTOR, NATURAL DISASTER AND THINGS ARE MEANINGLESS.

MORE FROM AL AT: microcosm.pub/ALBURIAN

MICROCOSM PUBLISHING IS PORTLANDS MOST DIVERSIFIED PUBLISHING HOUSE AND DISTRIBUTOR WITH A FOCUS ON THE COLORFUL, AUTHENTIC AND EMPOWERING. OUR BOOKS HAVE PUT THE POWER IN YOUR HANDS SINCE 1996, EQUIPPING READERS TO MAKE POSITIVE CHANGES IN THEIR LIVES AND THE WORLD AROUND THEM WITH BOOKS AND BOOKETTES ABOUT DIY SKILLS, FOOD, BICYCLING, GENDER, SELF-CARE AND SOCIAL JUSTICE. Subscribe to everything we publish! ➡ microcosm.pub/bff